Patty Bousa
&
Delbert. _
Please Return

BUILDING
SELF-ESTEEM

D1712134

**Also in the Aldersgate
Dialog Series**

BUILDING
SELF-ESTEEM

Published for the ALDERSGATE ASSOCIATES
By Beacon Hill Press of Kansas City
Kansas City, Missouri

ALDERSGATE

Gene Van Note
Editor

Patti Reynolds
Editorial Assistant

ISBN: 083-410-8364

Quotations from the following versions of Scripture are used by permission:
  The Holy Bible, New International Version (NIV), copyright © 1978 by New York International Bible Society.
  The New American Standard Bible (NASB), © The Lockman Foundation 1960, 1962, 1968, 1971, 1972, 1973, 1975, 1977.
  The Living Bible (TLB), © 1971 by Tyndale House Publishers, Wheaton, Ill.
  The New Testament in Modern English (Phillips), Revised Edition © J. B. Phillips 1958, 1960, 1972. By permission of the Macmillan Publishing Co., Inc.
  The Revised Standard Version of the Bible (RSV), copyrighted 1946, 1952, © 1971, 1973.
  The Amplified New Testament (Amp.), © 1958 by The Lockman Foundation.
  The New English Bible (NEB), © The Delegates of the Oxford University Press and The Syndics of the Cambridge University Press, 1961, 1970.

Cover Photo: Harold M. Lambert
Photos: 6, 23, 33—Wallowitch; 15—Hedgecoth Photographers; 40—Camerique; 72—David Hiebert; 79—Rising Hope

Contents

Chapter 1

Have You Looked in Your Mirror Lately?

by Craig W. Ellison

Background Scripture: Genesis 1:26, 31;
1 Samuel 16:7; Psalm 32:1-5; Colossians 3:10-17

At least once a day you look at yourself in a mirror. The last time you looked, did you like what you saw? Or did you see only wrinkles, blemishes, and faults that made you want to turn out the light?

We're surrounded by mirrors. Each time we look we have a chance to feel good or bad about ourselves. These mirrors are other people. They describe us. They make judgments about us. They accept us or reject us. They give us feedback about ourselves that we take to heart. In many respects, we become what the mirrors of people important to us say we are.

Everyone has a mental picture of himself or herself. We see ourselves descriptively—we're tall, female, white, middle class, a businessman. These labels make up our self-concept. We also think of ourselves evaluatively. We feel good or bad about our characteristics. Being tall may be good or bad; being female may be positive or negative.

Take Roberta, for instance. She is an attractive, bright girl. But as you get to know her, you discover a person who seems to lack self-confidence. Upon further examination you find that she was the firstborn in a family where the father intensely wanted a boy. Roberta has overheard her folks make comments about how they really wanted a Robert, but had a girl instead. The result has been that she has never felt accepted by her parents—and has never accepted herself for who she is.

Or consider Bill. He is tall, but physically frail. Both of his parents were athletic and placed great value on participation in competitive sports. Although Bill has done extremely well in school and has begun to move up the job ladder, he still has a nagging sense of doubt about himself. Somehow he feels like a failure. Most likely this is due to the fact that Bill was never able to meet his parents' expectations because of his lack of physical prowess.

Whether we feel good or bad about ourselves makes up what psychologists call self-esteem. Whether we have positive or negative self-esteem depends on how well we stack up against the characteristics we've learned to value most. We learn those values from our parents, friends, the media, employers, and teachers.

Throughout life, people affect the way we feel about ourselves. They do it by what they say. When people that we like or respect tell us, "You're neat. I like you!" we learn to value ourselves. But when we hear, "Can't you get anything right?" we feel bad about ourselves.

People also influence us by what they do. If people we like seem to want to spend time with us, that makes us feel good about ourselves. On the other hand, maybe everybody carefully moves away from us when we enter a room. Madison Avenue constantly exploits this need for acceptance through hair, toothpaste, perfume, and deodorant commercials on TV and in the print media.

The more highly we value someone, the greater impact his or her assessment has on our self-esteem. A close friend, spouse, parent, or boss may influence us tremendously. The more important the characteristic on which we're being evaluated, the more critical it is to us as well. I really don't mind if people think I can't tell one end of a bowling alley from another. It's just not that important to me. Usually we surround ourselves with people who like us for the characteristics that are central to us. That helps the probability that we'll receive support rather than suffer the psychological pain of being criticized.

The number of sources of evaluation that we have also affects the impact of any particular person's evaluation. Very young children have few sources besides their moms and dads. What Mom and Dad say and do toward them in their early years have an immense impact on how they will feel about themselves. The same is true for people who have very few friends, or mothers of young children who have very little out-of-home contact with other adults. What those friends or that spouse communicates about his or her worth assumes tremendous importance.

The values that our society prizes and passes on through education, media, and most parents are focused mostly on externals. How we look, what we own, and what position we have are critical. They determine our value. If we are beautiful, live on Chicago's Gold Coast, own a Mercedes Benz, and are a vice-president of a growing company, we're really okay!

But if, on the other hand, we're ugly or have the wrong skin color, are poor and unemployed, watch out! Nobody esteems us. In a society like ours that prizes appearance, acquisition, and achievement, it's tough to prize ourselves if we don't meet those standards. Remember the aerospace layoffs of a few years ago? Formerly confident, assertive, smiling, successful men with apparently unshakable positive self-esteem became depressed, doubting, and suicidal after months of being laid off from their jobs.

We see, then, that how we feel about ourselves is important. It affects our relationships, our careers, our emotions, and our behaviors. People who feel bad about themselves are more likely to have emotional and social problems. They're more easily hurt by others. They're more likely to have psycho-somatic illness and become delinquent. In contrast, people with more positive self-esteem are less sensitive to criticism. They can give and receive love better They're more curious, perform better, and are more likely to become leaders.

Now I don't think that, as Christians, we should make self-adjustment or self-actualization our idol. But God does want us to be trophies of His grace. Because of that He has given us some important guidelines for living which help produce, as a by-product, positive self-esteem.

Although the people we encounter are "mirrors," the Word of God also is a mirror. It reflects back to us how we fit God's ideal. It highlights our spiritual and moral acne, but it doesn't leave us feeling unable to approximate that image. The Word of God provides instructions as to how to get rid of our "acne."

The contrast between society's foundation of self-worth and the biblical base for self-esteem is startling. It's like sand compared to rock. The societal foundation of self-worth is based on power and put-downs. Our eyes are turned to things and people. We're always comparing ourselves with others to see how we look. We're encouraged to put others down so we can look better. This gets us into an endless rat race. But Scripture turns our eyes to God. It bases self-esteem on love and the stable base of God's high acceptance.

Having said this, we need to realize that both Scripture and psychology recognize the importance of other people for our self-worth. Although the Scripture urges us to lift up our heads from comparison with others, it doesn't counsel us to forget about people altogether. On the contrary. In the very act of creating human beings God said, "Let us make man in our image" (Genesis 1:26).

We are social beings. Throughout the Old and New Testaments the importance of a supportive community is expressed. God knows we need each other. At the same time, He exhorts us to move beyond competition and comparison. He stresses the importance of love, acceptance, forbearance, and forgive-ness in our relationships (Colossians 3:10-17). We are to care for one another—not compete with each other. The result is mutual affirmation.

The church community is important, then, as a place of acceptance. Each individual is to be treated as important. Each is to be affirmed as a unique expression of God's creation. The Bible also reminds us that each person has special contributions to make to the Body (Romans 12). We need to emphasize that. Too often we act as though only preaching and music count. This encourages "spectator-itis," and robs people of the opportunity to both contribute to the Body and affirm their own worth.

Finally, the church community has tremendous possibilities as a place for competence-building in practical skills. Small groups could be held to teach basic social skills for the shy, for example. Or retired people could teach accounting, woodworking, and/or a variety of other subjects. This would help build confidence.

The foundation of self-esteem that the Scriptures provide goes beyond other people, however. The roots of self-acceptance are to be found in God's acceptance.

First, the Bible tells us that man looks on the outward appearance but God looks on the heart (1 Samuel 16:7). This relieves us of much of the strain that our society's emphasis on physique, possessions, and positions places on us. God isn't impressed by externals.

Second, we're told that God created us and evaluated the human race as very good (Genesis 1:31). God saw human beings as worthwhile.

Third, even when we turned against Him in sin, He continued to value us and provided the Redeemer, Jesus Christ. Because He loves us, we can love ourselves.

Now this doesn't mean that we can do anything we want to and expect God to keep smiling. Some people use the term *unconditional love* apparently to mean that. God's love is free, but He expects obedience and integrity. Violation of His standards will bring feelings of guilt and negative self-esteem (Psalm 32:1-5).

Some have argued that we need to get rid of guilt feelings.

People shouldn't be so morally sensitive, they say. In contrast, the Bible says we need to get rid of our sin. We need to confess and repent. Clearly the biblical way is more realistic. We don't have to construct elaborate defenses to hide our faults from ourselves (or others). We can look straight into the mirror of God's truth, see our sin and needs, and still experience His accepting love as we admit it and turn from it. The reason we often find it hard to admit our faults to others or ourselves is that we fear the pain of rejection.

One of the questions that often arises in Christian circles is, "Isn't self-esteem pride?" Or, "Isn't self-love sin?"

It is important to understand that pride involves a spirit of independence from God. It is an attitude of superiority over others. Often it camouflages underlying inferiority feelings. The person who is proud is self-centered. Everything is done in reference to how it makes him (her) look.

Humility, however, isn't that way. It is marked by openness to the opinion of others. The humble person is able to look at himself accurately even if he isn't always on the top of the heap. But humility is not inferiority. The humble person neither puffs himself up or puts himself down. Clearly, a healthy self-concept is most closely linked with humility.

The Bible does not teach that we should feel bad about ourselves or believe that there is nothing good about us, although in comparison with God, that's morally and spiritually true. Fortunately, God offers to redeem us and give us the value that was lost due to sin. We can stand (not crawl) before Him because of His grace. In terms of intellectual, athletic, mechanical, musical, and social abilities, we may have considerable talents and properly feel good about ourselves. People may like us and compliment us; we don't have to make them think that we're awful. The root of our self-esteem, however, should be gratitude for God's love and creative work in us that gives us the potential and opportunities to develop those capacities. Rather than competitiveness and destructive comparison with others, we can thank God continually for making us uniquely for His purposes (Psalm 139:13-16). As long as our fundamental attitude is gratefulness to Him, our feelings of self-worth will not be self-centered.

Having good feelings about ourselves should not, then, be considered sin. Self-centeredness, selfishness, and narcissism are sin. But more often than not these orientations arise from an inability to love oneself and from the need to keep trying to prove oneself because of the failure to accept God's evaluation and acceptance.

Think for a moment about the way Christ seemed to view himself. The Scripture encourages us to be like Him. This seems to incorporate both His humble servanthood and His accurate, healthy, positive self-regard.

The history of God's relationships with human beings is not one of manipulating empty-shelled robots who have no personality. He gives us personality and is able to work through us. We should constantly submit ourselves to our Heavenly Father.

God has made us social beings who have a need for acceptance from others. Their acceptance of us is important for our own self-acceptance. Furthermore, God has created us and loves us himself. He has provided guidelines for living which also result in positive self-esteem. These include confession and repentance for sin (integrity), and loving others in a supportive body of believers.

The Scripture views us as spiritually and morally helpless—but not as worthless. God has a high view of our worth, and encourages us to love ourselves. At all times, however, we should feel and express appreciation to God for making us the way He has and giving the opportunities to us which allow us to be competent and confident as individuals.

Reprinted by permission from *Christian Life* magazine. Copyright 1981 by Christian Life, Inc., Wheaton, Ill.

Chapter 2

Symptoms of a Lack of Self-esteem

by Jon Johnston

Background Scripture: Psalm 27:14; John 10:10;
15:11; Ephesians 2:10; Colossians 1:10-13;
2 Timothy 1:7

In his best-seller entitled *Psycho-Cybernetics,* plastic surgeon and psychologist Maxwell Maltz describes a duchess who was painfully self-conscious about a large hump on her nose.

After a bit of gentle persuasion, she reluctantly agreed to submit to the scalpel. Then came the big day when the bandages were slowly unwound, and the beautiful, finely sculpted nose was revealed to its owner.

To Maltz's surprise, his patient expressed no elation. In fact, if anything, her spirits were more downcast than ever. And thereafter, in spite of her facial change, the duchess continued to play the unenviable part of the ugly duckling—even refusing to look others in the eye.[1]

What was her problem? Put simply, she possessed a severely depleted self-concept—a serious lack of self-esteem. Her

measuring stick of self-worth registered near zero. And the drastic improvement of her appearance did little good.

Self-haters Anonymous

All of us encounter people who despise themselves. Some do so in spite of visible evidence that suggests their worth. These are people whose pangs of loneliness are most intense when they are surrounded by friends; whose financial insecurity is most acute when they are living in prosperity; whose fears are most haunting while they are being comforted and even applauded.

In effect, these individuals turn securities into insecurities, assets into liabilities. They perpetually "snatch defeat from the jaws of victory."

The tragedy of such a condition is echoed in the words of W. S. Gilbert, "You have no idea what a poor opinion I have of myself—and how little I deserve it."[2]

Whether based on evidence or not, persons who are convinced of their inherent worthlessness become locked into a self-defeating thought pattern that easily results in blurred mental vision, crippled faith, an inability to meaningfully relate with others, and a felt-need to grope for false sources of security.

Realizing this, it is imperative that we replace a nagging sense of low self-esteem with one that is healthy and helpful. But, this necessitates the acceptance of three essential ingredients:

1. Self-acceptance—seeing clearly who we are
2. Self-approval—living comfortably with who we are
3. Self-affection—being grateful for who we are[3]

How can we incorporate these vital elements into our lives? The first step consists of understanding the "red flag" symptoms of a poor self-image. To do this is to be fully alert to any condition that might require prompt attention.

With this in mind, we turn to a brief analysis of the symptoms.

Telltale Evidence

Just as a sore and raspy throat can indicate the presence of cold germs, and a clanky automobile engine can imply an insufficient quantity of oil, so there are certain symptoms that strongly suggest a condition of low self-esteem.

It is obvious that most of these symptoms surface in all of our lives at one time or another. And that is normal. It is only when they are excessive in intensity and duration that we should be seriously concerned. Only then are they to be considered as bona fide indicators of low self-esteem.

With this qualification stated, we now direct our attention toward some specific symptoms.

One key indicator of poor self-esteem is *an incessant*

craving for positive evaluations from others. Persons afflicted by this serious malady often resort to such things as voicing insincere compliments or faking compliance in order to evoke "strokes" or "warm fuzzies" from those who feel obligated to reciprocate in kind.

It is as though such individuals possess some sort of external thermometer of self-worth—one which provides instantaneous readout of others' reactions. Quite expectedly, their mood is likely to swing very quickly from the extreme of elation to that of total frustration.

These abrupt changes in temperament can be triggered by the slightest act, both real and imagined. We smile when hearing about the excessively self-conscious person who attended his first football game and became extremely depressed when the team huddled. Why? He thought that the players were talking about him.

By contrast, persons who regard themselves as worthwhile are stabilized by a kind of internal thermostat which regulates the effects of positive and negative feedback on the psyche. Such individuals are, as a result, neither made heady by compliment or devastated by insult. Their course is steady and their spirit remains confident. In spite of circumstances, they remain consistently characterized by the kind of "power, love and a sound mind" that Paul advocates in 2 Timothy 1:7.

Another symptom relates to the source of motivation. People suffering from low self-esteem are *primarily propelled into action by such negative factors as fear, guilt, and crisis.*

When self-image shrinks, the "I-can-do-it" feeling invariably subsides. As a result, innovation, creativity, and ambition fade. It is no secret that persons having a weak ego tend to be devoid of energy and courage. Also, their vision is frequently clouded by a fear that makes unfamiliar thought and behavior patterns seem threatening. With this in mind, it is easy to understand why such individuals typically lack a self-starter and lapse into apathy.

But, admittedly, everyone must experience some change. Just how do self-haters ever come to alter their lives? The answer is simple: they are pushed by circumstances that they believe to be a serious threat to their well-being.

We have all known those who only become responsible marital partners when pressured by a threat of divorce; who stopped overeating only after having a heart attack; or who quit driving recklessly after having a terrible accident. Most tragic of all are those who have awaited a crisis before entertaining the thought of accepting Jesus as their Lord and Savior (2 Corinthians 6:2).

On the other hand, the individuals who have a healthy self-image are actors rather than reactors. They choose to mold, rather than being molded by, their environment—regardless of the cost. To paraphrase Huxley, they can do what needs to be done, when it ought to be done, as it ought to be done. To them, it is always "Straight Ahead!" And their own inner aliveness provides their springboard for action. (See Colossians 1:11.)

Still another symptom of a lack of self-esteem is *the unwillingness, and perhaps even the inability, to give.*

Giving, whether it be in the form of money or love, usually entails the relinquishment of resources, and becoming more vulnerable to the recipient.

Those with a starved self-image find it very difficult to cultivate a generous spirit. They reason, "Anybody I give to will be that much better off, and I will be that much poorer. How much better it is for me to out-earn and out-accumulate others. Then, perhaps, I can convince myself that I am truly worthwhile."

As a result of this thought pattern, such persons tend to relate to others in the following manipulative ways:

1. Put them down—"You are below me and my kind."
2. Put them on—"I'll only let you see what I want you to see."
3. Put them off—"I'll keep you from me by avoiding an authentic relationship."[4]

Obviously, people are not warmly receptive to individuals who treat them with such blatant disregard. Instead, they are quite likely to respond by providing self-haters with additional negative feedback to digest which only serves to further compound their difficulties.

It is so ironic. By insisting on getting rather than giving, persons plagued with a depleted self-concept are shunning the very antidote needed for their improvement.

The old adage is right: You cannot sprinkle the perfume of generosity upon others without spilling a few drops on yourself. Truly, as the Master said, and demonstrated so convincingly, "It is more blessed to give than to receive" (Acts 20:35).

Another symptom is the *tendency to be excessively defensive*. Persons who doubt their self-worth commonly adopt a "protection" complex. The walls of their psychic castle are high and thick, and their guns are trigger-ready to blast away at any external movement that might signify encroachment.

The weapons of defense are many: argument, insult, rejection through body language, and even emotional withholding (e.g., giving the "silent treatment"). Such tactics are perceived as necessary for "holding off the enemy" at a safe distance. Should the latter penetrate too closely, he would surely detect just how weak and defenseless the self-hater really is. So, in effect, this is a game of calculated bluff, which is based on paranoia.

In addition, those haunted by self-doubt have an arsenal of weapons that they rely on to protect themselves from themselves. These are termed "defense mechanisms," and function to protect from the harsh, real and imagined, enemies of reality. Let's examine a few:

1. Rationalization—thinking up plausible explanations to excuse ourselves ("But everyone cheats on their income taxes.")

2. Compensation—stressing a strength to camouflage a weakness ("So what if you saw me read a pornographic magazine. Don't overlook the fact that I own five versions of the Bible and read them regularly.")

3. Projection—attributing our own unacceptable attitudes or behavior to others ("I'm sure you'll dislike that minister the way I do.")

19

4. Fantasy—daydreaming ourselves out of the real world ("When I'm bored, I just close my eyes and pretend that I'm on a beautiful Greek island.")
5. Displacement—venting aggressive feelings toward "safe" sources that aren't responsible for our plight ("Whenever I get this upset at my boss, I kick the dog.")

Although other defense mechanisms are commonly listed, the above seem to be the most frequently used.

Once again, please remember that the key word is *excessive*. At times, we all need such emotional shock absorbers to help us absorb the unbearable pain of reality. Brutal rejection by a loved one, shocking news about a terminal condition, failure associated with a crucial exam we took or a well-earned promotion that was supposed to be a "sure thing."

It is only when we habitually retreat to and are overly dependent upon such defenses that coping skills diminish (e.g., neurosis)—and the real world becomes seriously distorted (e.g., psychosis). When this occurs, our defenses become our undoing, just as desensitizing drugs often deteriorate the physical body.

Rather than glossing over our shortcomings or becoming aggressive toward our fellowman, it is highly preferable that we recognize our true Source of strength and protection. Psalm 27:14 spells it out in unmistakable terms: "Wait on the Lord: be of good courage, and he shall strengthen thine heart."

A final symptom directly relates to our perspective. Those who deny self-worth are, usually, *tangled in the quagmire of pessimism and fatalism.*

Carl Sandburg once said, "Life is like an onion. You take off one layer at a time, and sometimes you cry."[5]

Self-haters weep profusely within themselves, and the crying intensifies as they look at the deepest layers of their innermost person. What they see is not beautiful. For them, in effect, God has made junk—and they are it.

With such a perspective, it is little wonder that everything seems bleak and the capacity for joy is exterminated. Life, as Thomas Carlyle put it, seems like a "dreadful circle which goes around and around toward the hole in the sink."

Such persons fix their gaze upon the actual and completely disregard the potential. To hear them tell it, their fate is as fixed as cement; they are born to lose. And the future only offers more of the same, or worse.

In addition, such individuals cast gloom upon those with whom they work and live, as well as become barriers that block their own creative achievement and self-improvement.

In sharp contrast to these are persons who feel good enough about themselves to gear their thinking toward the positive. Such individuals prefer to describe the cup as "half full" rather than as "half empty." They choose to focus on the dough surrounding the hole in the doughnut rather than the hole itself. With a smile that bespeaks of inner peace, they are apt to say something like, "Even a broken clock is right twice a day!"

Christians have every right to look upon the bright side of life—to sense intense fulfillment in the present and to anticipate an incomprehendable reward in the future. Why? Because Jesus offered up His very life's blood (Romans 5:8) to provide His followers with a joy that transcends any temporary disappointment (John 15:11) and an abundant life that is eternal (John 10:10).

Ephesians 2:10 describes the Christian as God's "workmanship." Allow the full impact of that thought to sink in. The divine Creator considers us to be His masterpiece, which He proudly exhibits to a sinful and corrupt world. Why? Because of what His Son lovingly did on our behalf.

Once this great truth is grasped, our anemic self-image is nourished into new life. Doubts are quelled; inner strivings cease. And we find a deep and abiding rest.

1. Maxwell Maltz, *Psycho-Cybernetics* (Englewood Cliffs, N.J.: Prentice-Hall, Inc., 1960), p. 7.

2. Cecil G. Osborne, *The Art of Learning to Love Yourself* (Grand Rapids: Zondervan Publishing Corporation, 1976), p. 27.

3. Ibid., p. 34.

4. Jon Johnston, *Will Evangelicalism Survive Its Own Popularity?* (Grand Rapids: Zondervan Publishing Corporation, 1980), p. 44.

5. Osborne, *Art of Learning*, p. 11.

Chapter 3

You're Someone Special

by Bruce Narramore

Background Scripture:
Psalm 139:13-18; 1 Corinthians 12:4-7;
Ephesians 4:15-16; Hebrews 1:10-12

Once we are committed to seeing ourselves from God's perspective, we need to apply this commitment in a practical and comprehensive manner to our own self-concept. It is one thing to understand that we can love ourselves. It is another to apply this understanding to the specific situation and self-evaluation that we all must face. In this chapter, we will look at how we can apply the principle of self-love to some of our specific emotional needs. We will be looking at God's comprehensive provision for all aspects of our self-concept.

Psychologists generally agree that our self-image is made up of a number of thoughts and attitudes toward ourselves. We tend to think of ourselves as either competent or incompetent, lovable or unlovable, secure or insecure, worthy or unworthy. These attitudes vary from time to time, in relation to our performance and our own and others' evaluations of us. If we are doing well at school, home, or work, our self-confidence gets a shot in the arm. We walk a little taller and feel a little better about ourselves. If, however, we are doing poorly, the opposite

22

takes place. We become a little insecure and our confidence begins to sag. Similarly, if people praise us or our achievements, we feel better about ourselves. If they criticize or rebuff us, our confidence takes a beating. In other words, the portion of our self-image relating to confidence can become a little shaky.

There are four central ingredients in our self-image: (1) a sense of worth; (2) confidence; (3) security; and (4) love.

1. The first of these, a sense of dignity or worth, is the basic attitude about our significance or value. If we are aware of our worth, we are on the road to a strong inner sense of identity. We believe we are significant. We believe we are valuable and that we have a right to live. Without a sense of worth, we become discouraged or depressed and fall prey to feelings of guilt, worthlessness, and condemnation.

23

2. A second ingredient in our self-concept is an attitude of confidence. Confidence, which implies a basic level of trust in our abilities and a sense of inner strength, is the quality that enables us to reach out and try new tasks or tackle new challenges. It is the opposite of inferiority. When confidence is lacking, we feel tense, anxious, frightened, or insecure.

3. Closely tied to a feeling of confidence is our need for a feeling of security. Whereas confidence is more of an internal matter ("I can do it!"), security is more external ("Others can be trusted" or "The world is safe"). Security relates to our environment and our relationship to it. It reflects our assurance that the world "out there" is basically safe. We needn't fear an impending earthquake, financial disaster, abandonment, or attack. This doesn't mean that the world is always a beautiful place or that everyone can be trusted. But it means that we have had sufficient positive experiences with others to know that we do have friends we can depend on, that the whole world isn't bad, and that we don't need to live in constant fear of starvation, physical disaster, or some other impending doom. People without a sense of security are constantly worrying about these and other potential tragedies and are unable to feel comfortable and relaxed.

4. A final ingredient in our self-concept is the feeling of being loved. Perhaps more than any other, this is the central ingredient of a positive attitude about ourselves. If we are to be happy and go through life with a minimum of problems, we need an assurance that we are loved and accepted and that we belong. When this is lacking, we feel alone, isolated, and depressed.

Conditional Self-concepts

Our self-concept begins to be formed in infancy. If our parents valued and accepted us, we developed a healthy sense of worth. If they complimented us and encouraged us to try new things, we gained a sense of confidence. If they provided a stable and secure environment, we learned to feel secure. And if they loved us freely, we learned to love ourselves.

On the other hand, if our parents had difficulty tolerating

our weaknesses, this also affected our self-concept. If they were critical, easily frustrated, overprotective, or failed to communicate their deep sense of respect and love for us, we probably entered adulthood with mixed feelings about ourselves.

Human nature being what it is, no one enters adulthood with a totally healthy self-image. Every parent occasionally loses his temper and verbally attacks his child's sense of worth or undermines his feelings of security. Every parent occasionally criticizes, overprotects, or in some way undermines his child's developing sense of confidence.

These facts, coupled with our failure to live up to our own goals and expectations, mean that we all enter adulthood with a relative or conditional self-concept. Either our self-concepts are relative to our achievements and the recognition they bring or they are conditional—dependent on our achievements and the evaluations we receive from our parents and other significant people. We learn to accept ourselves if we are able to live up to certain expectations, and we learn not to accept ourselves unless others accept us.

Such a perspective affects our whole style of living. Using the sentence "I can like myself if . . ." as our given, we go on to complete the sentence with any number of things. "I can like myself if I am successful." "I can like myself if I am likeable." "I can like myself if I am talented." "I can like myself if I am a good parent." "I can like myself if I am a good Christian."

But we can never fully succeed in living up to these conditions of acceptance. As children, we were able to please our parents some of the time. And we were able to please ourselves some of the time. Even as adults, we like ourselves and feel worthy, confident, secure, and loved some of the time. But at other times, serious doubts about our significance and worth arise. Our self-criticism, based on the conditional acceptance we received in our formative years, catches up with us and we become dissatisfied with ourselves when our performance slips or we don't gain the emotional support we want.

This shifting foundation for self-esteem can have serious consequences, for unless we live up to our inner expectations, we cannot really be content with ourselves. And even when we are content, we can't feel totally at ease because we know that our performance could slip and our self-doubt and self-criticism would return. As Maurice Wagner puts it:

> Our self-concept may seem fairly stable when life's ebb and flow of problems stays within acceptable limits. Occasionally, however, a tidal wave of unexpected difficulties overwhelms us. It may be a surprise illness, the sudden death of a loved one, a business failure, or a marriage or family problem that we cannot handle. Out boat is about to split in the middle and take water. At these times of unusual stress we become conscious of how strong or how weak our inner security really is. We seem to get in touch with our inner selves best in times of crisis. It is then that we begin to reach desperately for some resource to hold onto, some relationship that is available and reliable.[1]

An Unconditional Self-concept

The only absolutely sure and safe foundation on which we can build our self-esteem is a knowledge of ourself in relationship to God. He is absolute and unchanging in character. While human values shift and sway and many things on earth change, God remains a solid source of identity. The Bible says, "In the beginning, O Lord, you laid the foundations of the earth, and the heavens are the work of your hands. They will perish, but you remain; they will all wear out like a garment. You will roll them up like a robe; like a garment they will be changed. But you remain the same, and your years will never end" (Hebrews 1:10-12, NIV).

This is one truth we can know. We can build our lives around the fact that God is God; what He promised, He will do. From this foundation, we can erect a strong and stable sense of personal identity. Our self-image does not have to rest on the shifting sand of our performance and it does not have to rely on the judgments and evaluations we receive from others. God takes care of the needs that arise from our self-concept.

We Are Worthy

Long before we ever experienced the impact of conditional acceptance or knew what it was like to fail and not like ourselves, God built into our genes a wonderful pattern for growth, fulfillment, and development. This God-given potential is the ultimate basis for self-esteem. With these carefully chosen words, David expresses God's ultimate foundation for our sense of value, significance, and worth.

> For Thou didst form my inward parts; Thou didst weave me in my mother's womb. I will give thanks to Thee, for I am fearfully and wonderfully made; wonderful are Thy works, and my soul knows it very well. My frame was not hidden from Thee, when I was made in secret, and skillfully wrought in the depths of the earth. Thine eyes have seen my unformed substance; and in Thy book they were all written, the days that were ordained for me, when as yet there was not one of them. How precious also are Thy thoughts to me, O God! How vast is the sum of them! If I should count them, they would outnumber the sand. When I awake, I am still with Thee *(Psalm 139:13-18, NASB).*

The infant in the crib is a product of God's handiwork. Although marred by sin, the design passed down through his genetic structure is straight from the hand of God. Made in God's image, according to His design, the infant has a wonderful, complex potential for physical, intellectual, spiritual, and social development.

We Are Competent

Next to the knowledge that God created us stands another pillar of our self-esteem—the awareness of our abilities and a sense of inner strength. This pillar speaks directly to our need for confidence; it is the knowledge that God gives unique talents to each of us. No two people are exactly alike. Yet every person who has ever walked the face of this earth has been given gifts by God. Paul puts it this way:

> Now God gives us many kinds of special abilities, but it is the same Holy Spirit who is the source of them all. There are different kinds of service to God, but it is the same Lord we are serving. There are many ways in which God works in our lives, but it is the same God who does the work in and through all of us who are his. The Holy Spirit displays God's

power through each of us as a means of helping the entire church *(1 Corinthians 12:4-7, TLB)*.

In a unique way, each of us has a broad range of capacities, attributes, and potential. While differing widely in the way our gifts fit together, we each possess a beautiful, complex arrangement of capabilities that forms the nucleus of our real self—the person God designs and intends us to be.

The apostle Paul again speaks of these capabilities when he writes, "We will in all things grow up into him who is the Head, that is, Christ. From him the whole body, joined and held together by every supporting ligament, grows and builds itself up in love, as each part does its work" (Ephesians 4:15-16, NIV).

Sometimes we forget this powerful truth and feel tense, anxious, frightened, or insecure. We focus so much on our weaknesses and failures that we forget our talents and gifts. But if we remember God's creation, we gain a truer realization of the talents we possess. This gives us a solid basis for a sense of confidence. The fact that God has given us gifts and the power to use them is an absolute and unshakable foundation for our confidence. If we are merely chance beings with no special origin or abilities, we would have to struggle continuously to find confidence and to demonstrate our talents.

But now we can be at peace. We can rest in the complete confidence that whatever God intends that we should do, He has given us the ability to accomplish. We can confidently reach out, trying new ideas and tackling new challenges. Paul writes, "I can do everything through him who gives me strength" (Philippians 4:13, NIV). And Christ says, "I am the vine; you are the branches. If a man remains in me and I in him, he will bear much fruit . . ." (John 15:5, NIV).

We Are Secure

The third ingredient, our need for a feeling of security, is closely tied to a feeling of confidence. Here again, Scripture lays out a rich and trustworthy provision.

Do you remember the 1972 Olympics in Munich, Germany, in which several Arab guerillas held five Israelis hostage? For hours, the world waited anxiously for word about the captives.

Finally it came: "They have all been murdered."

I will never forget the shock on the faces of the television newsmen. They sat in silent disbelief. Finally, after a long pause, one of them said, "There's nothing we can say at a time like this." Then he went on to indicate that we could only "hope and pray" that things would get better.

My son, Dickie, and I were watching that telecast together. We were both deeply touched at the tragic loss of life and the seemingly senseless conflict. But then, we discussed the situation. I shared with Dickie the origin of the Arab and Israeli nations and explained that Ishmael, the son of Abraham by his wife's maid, Hagar, was the father of the Arab people. Then we discussed the spread of the Israelites throughout the world and their eventual return to the Promised Land. I showed Dickie from the Bible that the current Arab-Israeli conflict is part of a centuries-long problem that will eventually culminate in the return of Christ to earth. I told him that these conflicts weren't going to cease; they would probably get worse. But in the end, God's plans would triumph. This biblical insight helped us to put the whole event into proper perspective and provided needed security during those troubled days.

In similar ways, the Bible sheds light on numerous perplexing events and happenings of our day. It is our one great source of security in the midst of the confusing happenings in our world. God promises us security in our relationship to Him. He promises that nothing will be able to separate us from His love (Romans 8:38-39). He is with us day by day and we will spend eternity with Him.

We Are Loved

The final ingredient in our self-concept is the feeling of being loved. Probably the best-known verse in the New Testament is John 3:16, which reads, "For God so loved the world that he gave his one and only Son, that whoever believes in him shall not perish but have everlasting life" (NIV). Here, in a nutshell, is the best foundation for a lasting attitude of self-love. Even before we were born, God chose us to be His children. The apostle Paul writes, "For he chose us in him before the creation of the world to be holy and blameless in his sight. In love he predestined us to be adopted as sons through Jesus Christ, in accordance with his pleasure and will" (Ephesians 1:4-5, NIV).

Just as the fact that God created us with unique gifts can provide us with a deep, abiding sense of worth and confidence, the fact that God loves and chose us can provide a lasting source of assurance. What a strong foundation for self-acceptance we have, because God has chosen us to be His sons! This acceptance doesn't come and go according to our performance. It is a love that is completely unconditional. As David puts it:

> Where can I go from Thy Spirit? Or where can I flee from Thy presence? If I ascend to heaven, Thou art there; if I make my bed in Sheol, behold, Thou art there. If I take the wings of the dawn, if I dwell in the remotest part of the sea, even there Thy hand will lead me, and Thy right hand will lay hold of me. If I say, "Surely the darkness will overwhelm me, and the light around me will be night," even the darkness is not dark to Thee, and the night is as bright as the day. Darkness and light are alike to Thee *(Psalm 139:7-12, NASB)*.

God's love is unconditional. No matter where we go or how we do, God's love for us remains consistent. He is always present with us.

When the four ingredients of the positive self-concept are lacking, we suffer from the influence of an inadequate self-concept. Since each area of our self-concept has an opposite, we experience a negative emotion for every positive attitude that is missing. The ingredients in these two self-concepts, then, are:

Positive Self-concept	Negative Self-concept
Sense of Significance and Worth	Feeling of Badness, Worthlessness
Attitude of Confidence	Anxiety and Feelings of Inferiority
Feelings of Security	Insecurity and Worry
Awareness of Being Loved	Loneliness, Isolation, and Depression

The Christian's Choice

Now we can see that there are two possible directions for us as we attempt to establish self-esteem. The first direction says, "I can like myself if others like me," "I can like myself if I live up to my goals and expectations," "I can like myself if I succeed in avoiding feelings of guilt and condemnation." In other words, we can choose to build our self-love and self-acceptance on our performance and others' evaluations of us. We can decide to operate on the basis of a conditional or relative self-concept.

The problems with such an approach are obvious. Constantly under pressure to perform, we must earn our acceptance. We must prove our worth and we must succeed in order to develop confidence. We must keep on looking for security. Although this is the approach we all use to some degree, it is an inadequate approach to self-acceptance.

By contrast, we can decide to establish our self-concept on the absolute and unchanging God of the universe. With Him, our worth is not conditional. We don't have to work to prove our competence or do anything to merit love, for our security is rooted in Him.

The first approach attempts to earn self-esteem through works. The second approach is based on God's grace. The first is built on comparison and competition. The second is available to all. How can we ever have a strong and lasting sense of self-esteem if it is dependent on our achievements and acceptance? If we judge ourselves on the basis of performance, one-half of the people are destined to be losers. They can never measure up. But God didn't design this type of system. In God's system, everyone is entitled to dignity and worth. We are entitled to confidence and strength. We are all entitled to a feeling of security and lasting love. And it is God who provides for our needs of worth, confidence, security, and love.

1. Maurice Wagner, *The Sensation of Being Somebody* (Grand Rapids: Zondervan, 1976), p. 103.

From *You're Someone Special,* by Bruce Narramore. Copyright © 1978 by the Zondervan Corporation. Used by permission.

Chapter 4

Building On Failure

by Barry Bailey

Background Scripture: Mark 14:66-72; 16:7

One of the most significant aspects of the Bible is its honesty; it deals with the genuine. Regrettably, it is often introduced to us as a religious book, and we fail to grasp its authenticity. The Bible is not a promise of the religious success that follows faith but the candid history of people struggling for faith.

With this quality of the Bible in mind, let us look at Simon Peter's story. On the last night of Jesus' life on earth, Simon Peter was there. He was following Jesus at a careful distance, though to his eternal credit, Simon Peter was present—most of Jesus' other disciples were not. While they were standing beside a fire, a young woman turned to Peter and said, "You're one of His disciples, aren't you?" And Peter replied, "I don't know what you mean." Someone else said, "You are one of His disciples. You're a follower of that man!" Then, the third time it happened, Simon was angry and lashed back with an oath, "I don't even know what you are talking about. I don't know Him at all." And at that moment, the cock began to crow. In

Peter did exactly what we must do at times—he wept bitterly.

Luke's account, Jesus then turned and looked at Simon Peter, who remembered Jesus' prediction about the denial, and Simon Peter went away and wept bitterly.

Doesn't that story describe some characteristics similar to our own? We pride ourselves on our loyalty and steadfastness. We are boastful and often appear very sure of ourselves. But beneath all that, we can be rather disgusting people. We are weak; we can be egotistical and sinful. Often, we prove not to be dependable at all. We behave as Simon Peter did.

Peter's story does not stop here, however. A few weeks after his denial of Christ, this same man, Simon Peter, stood up to preach a sermon. Surely he was aware that someone would remember his earlier failure and say, "Who are you to speak to us? Why, you denied Him. Three times you said you didn't even know who Jesus was, and now you're trying to preach!" But I don't think that denouncement would have threatened Peter; he did not try to disregard that failure in his life. He never forgot it, we can be sure—he did not try to make a new beginning by wiping the slate clean. He was strong because he knew who he was. I think Peter would look us squarely in the eye and would say, "That's right, I denied Him. Yet now I'm asking you to follow Him, so that you can see what He can make of your life." That is not just great preaching; that is the heroic substance from which life is made!

Yet, look how artificial we are! When we have problems, we try to put them in the past in order to make a fresh start. It is very much like the way most of us make New Year's resolutions; we have grown up with the idea of wiping the slate clean and starting over again. "Let us have a fresh beginning!" and we pretend we did not do what we have done.

However, we are haunted by this falseness because we are not dealing with reality. We cannot really start over, for we are who we are. Even if we could literally begin again, we would not recognize ourselves. If we got rid of all our weaknesses, nobody would know us. We would be total strangers to ourselves and to one another.

There is a far better approach than starting over again. And that is building on what we already are—the good traits and the bad, our strengths and our weaknesses.

Let us look at several aspects where we are. For many of us, one impediment to doing so is that we major in our disappointments. Some people dramatize their weaknesses and cling to their failures. What if Simon Peter had talked only about his denial of Jesus? Suppose that every time he stood up to preach he had told that same story. Who would not have grown tired of it? And of him! We can weep with someone only so long—we run out of Kleenex after a while. If Peter had preached in that way, he would not have grown and his audience would have dwindled. But there are some of us who

34

are happy only when we are sad; we feel secure only when we are lost. We are determined to be more miserable than anyone else. We become caught in our failures.

Martin Luther was one of the great leaders of the church in the 16th century and is credited with being a founder of the Protestant Reformation. As a young Catholic priest, and before he was disassociated from the church he loved so much, Luther not only went to confession every day, he would have gone almost every hour.

On most nights, Luther slept well, but he felt guilty about it, thinking, "Here am I, sinful as I am, having a good night's sleep." So he would confess that. One day the older priest to whom Luther went for confession said to him, "Martin, either find a new sin and commit it, or quit coming to see me!"

Another barrier some of us encounter in starting where we are, is that we rationalize our actions so effectively that we do not realize that we ever do anything wrong. Generally insensitive to our own sins, we reason that those "little" wrong things we do are not serious. But if it is dangerous to cling to our wrongdoings, it is just as dangerous to be so well defended against our sins that we are unaware of them. We can be so convinced that we are good; the fact that we do not commit certain great sins gives us a false security, and we conclude that we never do anything wrong.

Jesus once turned to some people who were better than we will ever be at keeping the Law and said, in effect, "Quite frankly, the prostitutes are going to get into heaven ahead of you. At least they know what to confess. They know where their sin is." Goodness can so blind us that we think, "O God, it's so marvelous for You to have me in Your presence." If we are not aware of any of our wrongdoings, we will never find our true selves.

There is a third pitfall that is especially prevalent among those of us in the Church. Our problem is that we play the religious game; we want to be *so* religious. Jesus did not say, "Come, follow Me and be religious." Rather He asked us to find the truth. There is a difference! Did it ever occur to us that some of our efforts to be religious can make us blind to the truth. Those efforts are our attempts to use religion for our own ends by being manipulative or trying to control God. For instance, at a football game, each team may pray to win. According to some popular religions, both teams come onto the field, and the one that prays the best, wins. God does not have anything to do with such prayer. God answers prayer, but not like that—that is not how prayer works!

The manipulative religious game does not work. Simon Peter could have been religious in that sense. But notice how honest the New Testament is. It does not play down what Peter did, nor does Peter himself minimize his actions. We are not told that he was right or that he could start over by pretending that he did not deny Jesus. Three times Peter had said, "I don't even know who this Jesus is," and he had cursed. How would we like to have that reported about us in the newspaper, let alone in the New Testament!

When Jesus turned and looked at Simon Peter, we know what happened. Peter did exactly what we must do at times— he wept bitterly. That is better that wiping the slate clean and starting over again. That is better than a new beginning. God worked with Peter where he was, not through pretending to be where he was not. And because of that, Peter suddenly realized who he was. Until then he had been bluffing, playing a religious game, for he had said, in effect, "O Lord, don't tell me I am going to deny You. Look how good I am!" In that denial and in the aftermath, the whole Simon Peter was brought into focus. He would never forget who he was, and that was his power.

From the story of Peter we learn the power of starting where we are, and out of this knowledge, we can conclude three things. First, we ought to stop running from ourselves. Who are we trying to impress? People who know us and like us for what we are, already see us more clearly than we want them to. Who are we trying to fool? Simon Peter could have stood up each time he preached and said, "I want you to know how much I love Jesus." But that is not how he went about it— he told his story and let people see that the gospel can take a man who is weak and make him a rock. Simon began to reveal

36

who he was—to himself, and to other people.

So let us stop running from ourselves. If you are an alcoholic, admit it! You do not have to drink! If you have lied, you do not have to deny it to stop doing it. If you have hurt others, if you have been weak and self-destructive, do not lie about it. If any of us ever change, it will not be because we have pretended we did not do wrong. If we ever change for the better, it will be because we have had the audacity to recognize our weakness and to see who we are.

Additionally, let us realize from this story of Peter that our very weakness can help us to become strong. Our awareness of that is one of the reasons we appreciate Peter. We say that he is like we are. And when Jesus is pictured with some sense of accuracy, that is one of the things we like about Him: We are not excited by Jesus, the Child in the manger, as much as we are drawn to Jesus, the One who in all things was tempted as we are tempted. And remember when He turned to His disciples and said, in words something like these, "Are you going to leave Me, too? These other people followed Me, but now I am unpopular, and they have gone away. I did not expect everyone to stay with Me, but I thought you would." Seeing Jesus like that, we can relate to Him. He knew what it was to be hurt, to be disappointed, to cry. He was real!

We are slow to learn this lesson—we think that we are worthy and lovable only when we are strong. But we are wrong. A show of strength is often merely a form of bluffing. We find true strength when we put aside pretense and are open and honest. That is when power begins. I am not suggesting that we overconfess our sins, as Luther did. Nor am I suggesting that we do our dirty laundry in public—that would be foolish. But if we are introduced to ourselves as we are, then our very honesty about our weakness helps to make us strong.

That was true in Paul's life, certainly. Probably the greatest statement ever made about love was made by Paul, to the church at Corinth. He was the greatest missionary of all time. But consider his former life. He had changed his name; there was a time when he was known as Saul. It was he who had held the coats of the men who stoned Stephen, that first martyr of the church. What would we think of one of our ministers who played that role?

Paul surely never forgot that experience, but he did not start over again and put the event out of his mind. Rather, he referred to himself as the greatest of sinners. But the gospel takes hold of that sort of man and molds him. So the day came when Paul could write about love. No wonder; he had experienced it! The very thing about ourselves that we despise and hate—the very same weakness that can wreck us—can help to make us strong! I believe that with all my heart.

Finally, a third thing we can learn from the story of Peter is that we can start where we are because we are accepted, just as we are, by God through Christ. We are not loved by God in order to make us better, but because of who we are now. When we really like a person, we like that person just as he or she is. Oddly enough, though, our love will help to bring that change about. But we do not love the person in order to make that happen. We simply love that person.

God made His world and He never left His world. Jesus was born into this world—that is the Incarnation. God knows us exactly as we are; we need not bluff any longer. God does not play tricks with us by loving us to make us better. However, when we know that, we find that we do become better; we do live beyond our failure. We are loved and accepted as we are. Isn't that preferable to a multitude of new beginnings?

We should be glad that Simon Peter did not start over again. If he had, we might never have known about him. One day he stood up and preached; we call that day Pentecost. Some 5,000 people were brought into the fold of the Early Church. That is powerful preaching! What gave him the power to preach like that? He remembered a night when he had said, "I don't even know the man!" And that weakness, realized and recognized in the light of God's acceptance, helped to heal him. That is far better than trying to wipe out a mistake and pretend that it did not happen. God did that for Peter—and God through Christ can do that with you in your life now.

From *Living with Your Feelings*, by Barry Bailey. Copyright © 1980 by Abingdon. Used by permission.

Chapter 5

GUILT—
Its Causes, Its Cures

by Paul B. Wood

Happy Love - is not love is choice but by will

*Background Scripture: Job 2:1-10;
2 Corinthians 5:17-18; Ephesians 2:14-16*

There is a great difference in feeling guilty and being guilty. Job learned this as a result of his being oppressed by Satan. As do many people, Job believed that he must be a bad person if so many terrible things were happening to him. In fact, though, he was oppressed because of his righteousness. For the time, however, Job felt guilty—and suffered immensely as a result.

Guilt is a feeling of despair, of worthlessness and of pain—a sense of having done wrong. It arises from the conscience, which is the punitive aspect of the superego—the internalized standards of society.

It is not true that conscience develops automatically. The potential for its development is built in, but it develops as a result of experience—usually by significant role models in the life of a child.

An absence of capability for feeling guilty tends to produce an individual who will be hopelessly unable to fit into society. He

not only has no social or individual conscience, he has no internal control.

Guilt feelings impel an individual to action—to do something to relieve the feeling. He may confess, do penance, or seek punishment in a variety of ways. Often he feels depressed and anxious.

Excessive, chronic guilt feelings are very likely to be disabling. Many physical problems result from this condition and many others are made worse by it.

In the life of a Christian, guilt feelings result in a life of compulsive self-doubt and spiritual defeat.

Feelings of guilt may arise from several sources. To take appropriate measures to deal with guilt feelings, it is essential to recognize their source.

Job had to confront God and "state his case" before he began to free himself from his dilemma. After he recognized that he wasn't guilty of unrighteousness, he began to see that he only felt guilty. He was both oppressed and depressed. He discovered this simple yet profound truth: to be guilty is one thing; to feel guilty is quite another.

Many contemporary "Jobs" need to learn this lesson.

Why is it so hard to recognize the source of guilt feelings?

One problem is that guilt feelings may not be directly related to any current behavior. They may arise from those hidden aspects of the personality—the "unconscious."

Most of us have had the experience of awakening after a night's sleep feeling depressed and guilt-ridden. I am convinced that these feelings may be a result of something we have dreamed during the night. Often the dream is forgotten by the time we are fully awake. These dream-initiated feelings of guilt persist into wakefulness.

St. Augustine, in his *Confessions,* wrestled with this very problem. For him it was more than a question of feeling guilty. He remembered his dreams and felt that he was responsible for them—therefore guilty. When God revealed to him that he was not responsible for his dream "actions," he was able to conquer his feelings of guilt and despair.

Unconscious conflicts may be responsible for the overwhelming sense of guilt that is often a part of grief reactions.

Most Christians have a realistic understanding of death at an intellectual level. At an unconscious, emotional level, however, it is often a different matter.

When a loved one dies, all the old, repressed, negative feelings about that person may be reactivated. Many of these feelings arise from childhood memories and conflicts and are unacceptable to the conscious, rational, and Christian mind. They aren't consciously experienced, but unconscious feelings that are aroused leak into awareness. Despair comes into conflict with the Christian hope and doubts arise. As a result people may accuse God or question their own experience with Him.

These are some of the unfortunate consequences of unconsciously produced guilt feelings.

In considering sources of guilt feelings, it is necessary to point out that they often appear because a person is guilty.

These feelings are moral guiltiness, a realistic awareness that one is guilty of sin—a violation of God's law.

Conviction for sin is based upon an awareness of guilt and is normal and desirable. "Conviction" of guilt is, to some degree, universally found in man.

A sense of guilt as a result of sin has psychological and spiritual implications. Sin has eternal consequences, a fact which brings even greater hopelessness and despair.

Modern man has developed elaborate means of rationalizing about sin in an attempt to relieve guilt. Psychologists have explained that all behavior results from impersonal forces that mold personality. No one is responsible for his behavior, they say. Behavior is determined by heredity and environment. They ask how a person can feel guilty for something for which he does not feel responsible.

But man is responsible! He knows it.

In the vast array of possible behaviors that confront people are choices that are either right or wrong by some standard or other. Even unenlightened individuals have an innate sense of obligation to some higher law or authority.

The interesting fact is that now the concepts of sin and responsibility are reappearing in psychological circles—concepts that find their meaning in a moral consciousness and a capacity for guilt. Unfortunately, psychologists are not the only ones who have attempted to rationalize sin and guilt away. Some theologians and preachers have done the same.

I believe that, as a church, we need to reaffirm the concept of sin and guilt so that we can point the way to the Cure.

Moral guilt is easily relieved. Not by rationalization, though. Rationalization may mask guilt, to a degree, but it does not truly relieve guilt.

The remedy is as old as the atoning death of Christ and His resurrection. Reconciliation to God—through confession and repentance—totally negates the guilt. A forgiven person is no longer responsible for his sins. God has removed them, erased the slate, buried them in the deepest sea, and made them of no consequence. A genuine realization of this fact will do more than save a person. It will have a profound effect on his feelings of guilt.

It is difficult to imagine anyone refusing to deal thus with the problem of guilt. Confess, repent, and stop sinning. It's that simple—perhaps too simple for sophisticated modern man.

Recently I saw a bumper sticker which declared, "Christians Aren't Perfect—Just Forgiven."

I have no intention of discussing the concept of Christian perfection, but the obvious fact is that none of us are free from error. If we aren't perfect, we are sure to be aware of our imperfections. This can result in guilt feelings—or personal guilt.

Personal guilt may result when we don't reach our own personal standards. Of course, when these standards are God-given personal convictions, violation constitutes sin.

Many individual standards are not necessarily God-given. Though standards may be acquired through learning, either direct or incidental, some of them may be thought of as tradition or as "local rules." Some may be "Aunt Susie's notions." Though they are often peculiar and difficult to understand, standards are essential in human society if only to lend a sense of continuity and predictability to our lives.

It is important to understand that God's expectations for us are fair and reasonable. God will lead us into a clear understanding of what He requires of us.

It may be necessary to discern which standards we are imposing on ourselves are in fact God's standards.

There are ways to measure, examine, and understand these rules. For instance, do they contribute to spiritual growth? Do you have more rules on things, schedules, and other externals than on spiritual and devotional matters? Is the way you look more important to you than your prayer life?

Sometimes our rules have little to do with the essentials of the spiritual life. God wants to give us an understanding heart as well as an obedient one.

"Confessing your faults one to another" is good, but majoring on our imperfections is probably not conducive to spiritual growth. Insight is a most useful tool to aid spiritual growth.

A guilt feeling that rises from a deep-seated sense of badness has nothing to do with our behavior, though our behavior may be affected by it.

I'm not talking here about guilt which results from man's essential depravity—or original sin, either. Both of these guilt problems are taken care of through the Atonement. I am talking about a deep-seated sense of badness for which there is no explanation.

A sense of worthlessness seems to be ingrained in some people—it might even be considered a personality trait. These persons may be completely circumspect in behavior, yet they feel guilty. To use an old expression, "They never get the victory."

Nonspecific guilt feelings can create more problems than specific ones. With fear, for instance, we know that it is preferable to be afraid of something than of nothing. So we attach our nonspecific fear to some specific object or situation to make it more tolerable—less threatening.

A similar thing can happen with guilt. People often misbehave in order to have an explanation for their guilty feelings. Obviously, this could be very spiritually defeating.

This condition can be very destructive to the Christian life. It may lead to the "chronic seeker syndrome." The individual confesses his sins and believes—at an intellectual level—that

God can and will forgive them. Soon, however, the same pervasive sense of guilt rears its ugly head, and he concludes that he was never forgiven. After all, good people don't feel guilty (say we, said Job, and says the devil).

The question is how to deal with this particular problem of guilt.

Perhaps Job's solution would help. To paraphrase, "I feel guilty of sin, but God and I know I am not guilty."

It is appropriate for us to feel good (even proud) of the righteousness that is imputed to us by God. What God has made is right and good. Can it be pleasing to Him for us to act as if His plan of redemption isn't adequate?

The redeemed of the Lord should feel like it. It's scriptural: "But let every man prove his own work, and then shall he have rejoicing in himself alone, and not in another" (Galatians 6:4).

Guilt, then, can be good and helpful or it can be counter-productive and destructive.

The most important guilt with which to deal is that which comes from the problem of sin. Confess, repent, and stop sinning. This will do more to give us power to cope with the problem of guilt than any other thing we can do.

Our covenant with God needs to be renewed daily. We need to ask Him to direct our lives, to give an assurance of His forgiveness and acceptance.

Have sense enough to know that you aren't perfect. This will prepare the way for spiritual growth, and spiritual growth will minimize our shortcomings.

Seek God's standards for your life. Recognize that His rules are reasonable, individual, and not burdensome to follow. Commit your humanness to His mercy and understanding.

God loves us even when we are our worst. Surely He loves and accepts us when we are doing our best. If you have a pervasive sense of badness that you may have developed early in life, seek help. If you have honestly confessed your sins, God has forgiven and forgotten. If you still feel guilty you may need simply to recognize the difference in feeling guilt and being guilty.

From *Vista*, September 7, 1980, issue. Used by permission.

Chapter 6

Does Forgiving Take Time?

by David Augsburger

*Background Scripture: Romans 15:7;
1 Corinthians 13:5-8; Ephesians 4:32; Hebrews
12:15*

"Sure, I'll forgive that man, when I'm good and ready," the wife said as we sat around the kitchen table.

The forgotten teakettle whistled a forlorn note from its place on the old wood range. The man in question sat, eyes downcast, speechless before her anger.

"If you only knew the misery he's caused me, you'd understand why I'm not going to knuckle in when he says 'Sorry' for the first time," she continued. "Sure, I'll forgive him, but not until he's paid for a bit of the dirt he's dragged us through."

He stole a glance at her; and the air, hanging heavy with hostility, hit you in the face like high humidity. Then we sat in silence. I could see by her mobile face that she was reliving one of the many scenes of combat that had happened here in this kitchen.

Or was she recalling the day a week before when she and her daughter drove into town to trace down and threaten the

woman—"the other woman," as the pulp magazines always put it.

They rang the doorbell and waited. Then the woman stood framed in the screen door, squinting out the bright daylight, slowly recognizing who her callers were. Her knuckles glinted white on the doorknob. Her face an impassive mask. They stood mute in mutual hate.

Then the daughter broke it. "I've wanted to see your face for years," she said, "and now that I've seen it," she continued, and spit on the ground, "you make me sick."

"Oh, no, I'm not knuckling under," the wife said again as she got up from the table. "He can come crawling on his knees for a change."

Years passed; the other woman had married and moved out of his world. Slowly, bitterly he paid, repaid and overpaid for all he'd done. At last, one night when she herself was deep in trouble, lonely and bitter, she offered her forgiveness. Too late.

"You can keep your phoney forgiving," he told her. "I don't need any of it now. I've paid through the nose for what I've done. Who needs forgiveness when he's already paid?"

Who indeed? Forgiveness is a free gift of love or it is nothing of value. It is never a receipt for payment in full. It's an undeserved pardon. An unwarranted release.

When it's postponed until the last angry installment is collected, complete with bitter interest, it's pure vengeance.

If you hold back forgiveness until the offender deserves it, forget it! That's not forgiveness!

Forgive immediately!

Forgive when the first hurt is felt!

The man who follows Christ in life hurries to forgive. Quickly. Unhesitatingly! Immediately!

Knowing the great value of time, he cannot afford to let it slip by in futile pain.

He knows it is cheaper to pardon than to resent. The high cost of anger, the extravagant expense of hatred, and the unreasonable interest on grudges make resentment out of the question!

He forgives before the sting has begun to swell; before the

molehill mushrooms into a mountain; before bitterness, like an infection—or rigor mortis—sets in!

What a strange thing bitterness is!

It breaks on us when we need it least, when we're down and in desperate need of all our freedom, ability, and energy to get back up!

And what strange things bitterness can do to us. It slowly sets, like a permanent plaster cast, perhaps protecting the wearer from further pain but ultimately holding him rigid in frozen animation. His feelings and responses have turned to concrete, and, like concrete, they're all mixed up and firmly set.

Bitterness is paralysis.

A young man, falsely accused, condemned and penalized by his high school principal, turns sullen, angry, bitter. His faith in all justice and authority dies. He will not forgive.

A girl, betrayed by a fellow she trusted, is forced, becomes pregnant, then turns bitter and withdrawn. Her faith in all humanity ends. She cannot forgive.

A woman, deserted by her husband, left to be both mother and father to their two sons, turns angry at life—at the whole universe. Her faith in God and everything good has ended. She did not forgive.

Bitterness is such a potent paralysis of mind, soul, and spirit that it can freeze our reason, emotions, and all our responses.

So why do we accept bitter feelings? Why do we nourish acidic emotions and slowly allow them to eat away our attitudes, motives, and even our spirits? The bitters come in so many varieties.

There's the I've-been-used-and-abused brand of bitterness that lets us stew in our own anger juices when we have no chance to vent these hostilities on the persons who've hurt us. So we take it out on ourselves.

Or there's the everyone's-against-me, nobody-cares kind of bitterness that grows into a full-blown martyr complex. Complete with self-pity and all that.

Or it may be the I'm-being-neglected-forgotten-and-over-looked routine of the housewife who's glowingly bitter over

49

being trapped in the house all day long with whining toddlers, endless chores, and a husband "out all day in a fascinating world."

Or it may be the blind curse-it-all-I'd-rather-be-dead bitterness that follows tragedy, grief, or failure, if we withdraw into ourselves in desperate despair.

We live in a world infested with all these and many more strains of bitterness, and unless we are highly resistant, we too will be infected. Again and again.

When it affects our emotions, love may turn to instant hate. And what's worse, both love and hate can soon sour to apathy, indifference, and cold neutrality. Bitterness cuts the nerve to our emotions. They go dead—like paralysis.

When it finally affects mind and reason, our attitudes turn cynical, uncaring, critical, and caustic. Where we once ventured to place faith in others, now we trust no one. Optimism darkens to pessimism. Faith grays into doubt.

We withdraw, turtlelike, into our protective shells of bitter distrust. We've been burned once—and once burned we become twice shy.

Letting bitterness seal us in can be just an excuse for acting irresponsibly. Being responsible in any painful situation usually calls for us to accept a bit of the blame for the way things are. But being bitter about it can save all that. We can scapegoat it all on others. We may even feel justified in blaming God for all our troubles and difficulties. (Remember? That was one of the first sins. Man's first impulse when in his first trouble. Blame God. Adam blamed the woman first—and then the Lord.)

What is the key to finding release from the paralyzing powers of bitterness? Turn your eyes outward. Stop thinking about yourself. Don't tolerate those thoughts of self-pity. Don't permit those angry thoughts of self-defensiveness to master you.

Doesn't our bitterness spring from our self-centeredness?

What a helpless, hopeless cycle of feelings bitterness brings. It carries us around and around the same senseless circle. Around and around ourselves. Like a child learning to ride a bicycle, knowing how to ride but not how to stop, we pedal on and on, afraid to quit, yet wishing desperately for someone to come and take the bars, break our circle, and let us off.

Only forgiveness can do that for us. Only forgiveness can intercept our endless orbiting around ourselves and set us free. Here's how the Bible describes it:

> Let there be no more [bitterness], no more anger or temper, no more violent self-assertiveness, no more slander and no more malicious remarks. Be kind to each other; be understanding. Be as ready to forgive others as God for Christ's sake has forgiven you *(Ephesians 4:31-32, Phillips)*.

Only the immediate kind of forgiveness God showed us in Jesus Christ can sweeten our bitterness and bring tenderhearted healing. It can even grub out "the root of bitterness" down in our personalities so that it will never again spring up and grow (see Hebrews 12:15).

Forgive immediately. Not just because it's safest for your own selfhood and sanity, but for the deeper reason—it is the way of Christ.

Christ's way was the way of giving forgiveness even before asked, and even when it was not or never would be asked by the other.

While His enemies were driving spikes through His hands, again and again, with every blow, He probably prayed, "Father, forgive them." That's forgiveness. Unasked, undeserved, yet freely given.

To think that we needn't forgive until we are asked is a myth to be punctured!

Forgive immediately! And then—forgive continually.

Live your forgiveness as a way of life. Constantly and consistently.

To live forgiveness is to give wholehearted acceptance to others. There is no forgiveness without genuine acceptance of the other person as he is.

But it is more than a shallow acceptance which is nothing more than tolerance.

"Open your hearts to one another as Christ has opened his heart to you," Paul wrote to the Romans (Romans 15:7, Phillips). To do this is to accept another in a way which takes real responsibility for the other. It is an accepting love which gets its sleeves rolled up and its hands dirty in helping, serving, lifting, and changing other's lives into the full freedom of forgiveness—God's forgiveness and man's.

Forgiveness is not leaving a person with the burden of "something to live down"; it is offering him someone to live with! A friend like you.

But the greatest test of continual forgiveness is the daily kind of forgiving love which gives and takes, freely accepting the bruises and hurts of living. No matter how difficult the blows life deals us.

For example: overwhelming tragedy.

I've a very dear friend whose oldest son—a fine, clean, brilliant boy—was suddenly killed in an auto accident one summer noon.

"I'm not going to take the quick, easy way of becoming bitter or rebellious about it," the father told me. "My son is gone. Someday we will meet again. In the meanwhile, I will be twice the man I would have been. Since he won't be here, I will try to do two men's lifework, his and mine."

And he is doing it. Turning tragedy to triumph, draining all its power to destroy him.

Another example: painful handicap.

Gen. William Booth, founder of the Salvation Army, tragically lost his eyesight. His son, Bramwell, was sent to break the news that there would be no recovery.

"Do you mean that I am blind?" the general asked.

"I fear we must contemplate that," his son answered.

"I shall never see your face again?"

"No, probably not in this world."

"Bramwell," said General Booth, "I have done what I could for God and for the people with my eyes. Now I shall do what I can for God and for the people without my eyes."

That is a complete absence of bitterness. That's facing the difficulties of life with the eager confidence of faith that excludes all self-centered resentment. That is living out your acceptance.

A greater test of living your constant forgiveness comes from the irritations of living with people. And forgiving—the constant give-a-little and take-even-more can do something even for personality conflicts.

The grease of forgiving love can reduce the friction and salve the irritation.

He rubs you the wrong way?

Forgiving love can eliminate the "wrong way." Nothing is impossible to him who loves!

Forgiving love,

> Has good manners and does not pursue selfish advantage. It is not touchy. It does not keep account of evil or gloat over the wickedness of other people. On the contrary, it is glad with all good men when truth prevails. Love knows no limit to its endurance, no end to its trust, no fading of its hope; it can outlast anything. It is, in fact, the one thing that still stands when all else has fallen *(1 Corinthians 13:5-8, Phillips)*.

You don't have it? You can! Come! Open your life totally to Christ. He is this kind of love! As you know Him more clearly, follow Him more nearly; then forgiving love will be yours!

Yes, forgive immediately, forgive continually, and then forgive—finally.

Forgive once for all. End it with finality!

Forgive forgetfully! It was said of Lincoln, "His heart had no room for the memory of a wrong."

Forgetting must follow forgiving.

To say, "I can forgive but I can't forget," is really saying, "I know how to overlook a wrong but not to forgive it."

Now, let's be clear. Forgetful forgiveness is not a case of holy amnesia which erases the past. No, instead it is the experience of healing which draws the poison from the wound.

You may recall the hurt, but you will not relive it! No constant reviewing, no rehashing of the old hurt, no going back to sit on the gravestones where past grievances lie buried.

True, the hornet of memory may fly again, but forgiveness has drawn its sting. The curse is gone. The memory is powerless to arouse or anger.

Not that the past is changed.

The past is the past. Nothing can alter the facts. What has happened has happened forever.

But the meaning can be changed. That is forgiveness.

Forgiveness restores the present, heals for the future, and releases us from the past.

Which leads us to the final goal of forgiveness.

Beyond even forgetting, there is healing! Reconciliation!

Forgiveness is not finally complete until the severed friendship is mended. And the new weld of depth-forgiveness should result in a deeper, stronger union afterward than ever existed before!

The final step in forgiving is go, do something to heal the wound until nothing remains but the forgotten scar.

Forgiveness is acceptance with no exception. It accepts not only the hurt you've received, it accepts the one who did the hurting, and it accepts the loss caused by the hurtful actions or words. It makes no exceptions. It is acceptance without exceptions. "Forgive as God for Christ's sake forgave you," Paul wrote (Colossians 3:13, paraphrase).

Forgiving is self-giving with no self-seeking. It gives love where the enemy expects hatred. It gives freedom where the enemy deserves punishment. It gives understanding where the enemy anticipates anger and revenge. Forgiveness refuses to seek its own advantage. It gives back to the other person his freedom and his future.

Have you found what forgiving like that can do to drive bitterness out of your heart? When once you've accepted the forgiveness Christ offers, when you've opened your whole soul to His forgiving love, He washes the bitters right out of you.

It brings new life to our withered hearts, new energy to our paralyzed emotions, new understanding to our frozen feelings.

And from there on, Christ gives you the strength to forgive. To give forgiveness and acceptance to others, no matter what may come. Or how often. It will hold up—even for the next 489 times. The whole 70 times 7!

From *The Freedom of Forgiveness,* by David Augsburger. Copyright 1970. Moody Press, Moody Bible Institute of Chicago. Used by permission.

Chapter 7

Harry Is a Welder

by James L. Johnson

Background Scripture: Acts 10:34-35;
Romans 8:16-17; 1 Corinthians 12:21-27

Harry is a welder. But a good welder. But he is still a welder. Nobody knows what a good welder Harry is, except Harry.

There comes that day when Harry, like so many others, views the parade of those who have become "accepted in the beloved," meaning to him that they are the cream of the crop in Christian culture.

On that day the missionary is put on a throne and figuratively bowed to as the personification of true destiny for the believer. Nobody intends that deliberately, but it comes across that way. The businessman sits and watches the "heroes of the faith" doted on, listened to, almost worshiped "for giving themselves to the call of God." But for Harry the welder the guilt begins to creep in. He has not made it.

He is not a missionary or a teacher or a preacher or the head of a Christian business. He is a welder. At that moment Harry begins to feel uneasy. A sense of false guilt is beginning

©VOLK

to take hold. He looks at his hands still showing the grime from welding, the grime that won't come off with soap. He dresses decently enough, but somehow it doesn't quite come up to the image of "successful, dedicated Christian worker."

Harry gives to missions and to his church from his hard-earned welder's money, but that won't quite suffice for the inner uneasiness about not making it himself in some level of "Christian service." Secretaries, typists, shipping clerks, truck drivers —name them. Many sooner or later go through this "How-did-I-miss-the-boat?" trap.

The situation becomes compounded when Harry hears about the "spiritual gifts"—such things as "the word of wisdom; to another the word of knowledge . . . to another the gifts of healing . . . to another the working of miracles; to another prophecy; to another discerning of spirits; to another divers kinds of tongues" (1 Corinthians 12:8-10). Or again, "And God hath set some in the church, first apostles, secondarily prophets, thirdly teachers, after that miracles, then gifts of healings, helps, governments, diversities of tongues" (1 Corinthians 12:28).

Now Harry doesn't feel he fits any of those. He is a welder. He ties steel together with flame! Where does that fit into the accepted levels of proper Christian work?

Harry's Mistake

So Harry makes his first mistake. He feels anxiety and guilt about missing out. He becomes highly introspective, trying to figure out why he is only a welder and not someone of much higher distinction in the Body. The introspection will lead him to try to allay his guilt by overcompensating for it. He will fling himself into every church activity he can. This he hopes will do two things: (1) make up for his missing "the call" earlier in life; and (2) evoke proper self-punishment for missing it, thereby balancing things out with God. Many a man has gone to extremes in joining every board meeting and every possible activity in the church in hopes of gaining favor with God. Somehow the "books must be balanced." So Harry does his best. And within a year he is totally exhausted.

This can all be compounded by someone asking, "And

Harry, what do you do?" How can he say he is a welder? Could he admit this in a group of teachers, missionaries, preachers, and Bible study leaders? Again, guilt.

He may now cover himself. "Well . . . I work in construction, or more like design work. . . ."

"Oh, what kind of design?"

"Well . . . I stitch pipe and rods together—"

"Of course! You're a metal sculptor!"

Harry isn't sure that is right, but it sounds good. At least it seems to impress everyone.

But when Harry goes home, his wife says, "Harry, you are a welder. Why be ashamed of it? Metal sculptor, indeed!"

That doesn't help either. Now Harry has left a false impression. More anxiety, more guilt.

Person Versus Personage

What Harry has done is put on a mask, but not his welder's mask this time. He has become a "personage," as Paul Tournier says in his book, *The Meaning of Persons*. Harry gave up his identity as a "person" to take on the "personage," which is a front to save himself from feeling anxious about not being "in" with the elite of Christian occupation.

Everyone has a "personage" or composite of who he or she is through life, environment, and expectation. As Tournier points out, the real person can get lost in the personage. The personage does his thing but hopes what comes out is acceptable. The person becomes lost behind it, and guilt may follow as the individual senses that he or she is not being honest.

"I cannot escape the danger," Tournier says, "of trying to show it when I have not got it, of covering up criticism and irritation under a mask of amiability, the discordance of which an intuitive person is quick to note. Is this then the price that has to be paid in every noble vocation? . . . The master must hide from his pupils the gaps in his knowledge. The barrister must show himself confident of success. The doctor would do grave harm to the morale of his patient were he to impart to him all his doubts about his diagnosis and prognosis. . . .

"If the eclipse of the person behind the personage has

taken on a new intensity in modern times," he goes on, "that is due to the technical development of our civilization, the concentration of the masses and the increasing mechanization of life. . . . The person is the original creation, the personage is the automatic routine."

What Harry did not understand is that "it is the calling that makes the person," including the welding. Instead he chose to be someone else, another person—to rise to the images he felt were proper ratifications of his Christian life. In doing that, he felt guilt, a false guilt.

It is difficult to blame anyone for this state of affairs. One could easily blame Harry and those like him who feel this way. But they are often left out, holding the bills that others run up in their "higher calling." But it comes down to Harry in the end. He will have to face himself as a true person, which means "Harry the welder" and not "Harry the metal sculptor." Perhaps he will simply have to back off trying to make up for it all by running the youth camp and driving the bus when it is only an attempt to compensate for what he is not.

It may well be that church organizations are creating their own measure of havoc by overemphasizing one form of calling over another. True, we should grant a salute to those who travel 10,000 miles to minister to some far-off tribe in the name of the gospel! Let's salute the preachers and the teachers for giving their all.

But somewhere Harry the welder needs a sense of ratification too. Because he "works for a living" is a poor distinction to lay on him. Because "he makes money" at his living is also a cruel devaluation. Perhaps no one outwardly says that. But it comes across all too often. There are the "called" and there are the "uncalled," and the "called" represent bona fide church work and service. The "uncalled" drive fire trucks and sell insurance and weld.

Growing into Guilt

The same sense of uneasiness and guilt creeps over the young, who are expected to rise to levels of "proper Christian service" because "you are attending a Christian college." Parents must take some of the blame for this. The students whom this writer has worked with for 15 years have openly confessed their guilt at choosing a "secular" job contrary to their parents' expectation. The tragedy is that they say, "But, you see, I have not been called." This means, "I have no aspirations to be a missionary, teacher, preacher, or whatever in a Christian institution as such." This may also mean that they are opting out of being a true Christian servant as manager of computer services or chief accountant at Sears.

The more serious complication in this is that they do feel a sense of anxiety in not rising to that "higher call." They have not faced it with God; they are too overwhelmed by the reaction of their parents or peers to consider that all of life's work can be given to Him.

One can even sense many times on Christian campuses a certain kind of division between those who are "bound for the mission field or some Christian service" versus those who are not really sure. Those who are not sure seem to group to themselves. They take on a form of the renegade, or think they do. In it all and over it all hangs a pall of guilt about not "making it."

Some students will try the personage route. They will talk the language, take on postures of spirituality, and seek to maintain a life-style that will prove they are "model" students in the Christian sense. They rise to the expectations of the institution at the expense of their own true personhood. They are inwardly aware of this mask, but it is their only means of negotiating the environment.

Thank God that Christian education is beginning to sense that each man and woman student must find his or her own way in God, regardless of the elitist groups that constitute the core of Christian service and even Christian culture. But the church and the institution must work much closer together in order to prevent the growing dichotomy that exists between "Harry the welder" and "Harry the missionary to the headhunters."

One man sensed this in his own son when he was 17 and contemplating a college. The man was a preacher. He naturally wished his son to follow in his footsteps. But because he was wise enough to know that laying this on him was forcing him into territory that God might not have for him, he said, "Roger, whatever college or career you choose is up to you. I know God will use you wherever you are."

This sounds simple, but at that moment, the father was bringing his son out from a tendency to rest on his personage into a sense of his real person. God finds it difficult to use the personage, but He uses the person with great effectiveness. When a person knows who he is and senses no need to cover for it, there is no need to play games.

But to be honest about all this is not easy. As John Powell said, "Most of us feel that others will not tolerate such emotional honesty in communication. We would rather defend our dishonesty on the grounds that it might hurt others; and, having rationalized our phoniness into mobility, we settle for superficial relationships."

But "Harry the welder" has to find his way back. The guilt trip has to end. The student must stop measuring himself by his more-spiritual peers—those with the "high callings"—and must recognize that he is unique and that in this uniqueness he is going to accomplish something for God that no one else can.

Grasping the Upper Echelons

And then there is the other tragedy: those who push themselves into the "upper echelon" in order to be accepted. These will drop their businesses in the secular world and work up a "call" to rationalize their taking on Christian work. This, they hope, will make them feel less anxious about "missing the boat." Students will put aside other career aspirations to be a missionary, convincing themselves that they are "called" to that. These people in the end become whirlwinds of unhappiness; they can't fit in because they were not supposed to be there in the first place.

This is the danger of creating emotional settings by which the very atmosphere forces an individual to shift from his personhood to a personage, to move from what he or she is and knows to be to a personage who will be acceptable. As Dolby says, "Emotions often can mislead because they are volatile, dependent upon physical and unconscious manipulations by ourselves and by others. It is easy to allow the emotions to overwhelm the rational processes, permitting a person to become victim of fickle whims."

The emotional highs of too many Christians bring them to the jargon of "I am having a mountaintop experience" or "I know I feel led by God to this or that place." Emotions have their place, because the gospel is emotional. But the danger for the individual is to use it to assuage guilt about not taking a certain course of action which is expected of him by others.

One can cite case upon case of people who have moved toward Christ in a highly charged emotional atmosphere. But many people are more concerned with doing what is expected of them than with acting out of sincere need. In this case the move is not to Christ but to the person controlling the emotional center of that meeting. When it is all over, that person feels even more confused—and worse yet, even more guilty.

Home but Not Happy

Housewives go through similar problems of this personage versus person. Wives who stay home because they feel it is scriptural feel guilty because they are not more active in community and church affairs. Never mind that there are young children in the house who need constant attention. Somehow that gets lost in the anxiety she feels in not "doing her thing for the kingdom." Some feel guilty because they are not leading a Bible study once a week. Some sense anxiety because others seem more active in Christian ministries.

Housewives often try to compensate in one or two ways: go out and start a career (which is all right, of course, but often creates tension with the spouse if there is not mutual agreement), or else plunge up to their necks in the church social whirl until they find it impossible to maintain a proper sense of order at home.

The Christian community simply lays too much on its own people with regard to what constitutes Christian service. A mother who feels constrained to give her children love and care at home should not be made to feel less "in" because she does so. Again, it is not enough to take a businessman's offering in the collection plate and not recognize his value in doing just that. It is likewise wrong to conclude that "money makers" are not spiritually the same as those who have become mobile in the territories of church outreach. When a pastor singles out certain people to be recognized—the teachers, missionaries, preacher's kids, and missionary's kids—as those who constitute some kind of "upper echelon," he must recognize the others as well—the carpenters, plumbers, salesmen, and secretaries as springboards to an outside world.

Unless that occurs, there will be this "personage-versus-person" syndrome going on in too many lives. As Tournier puts it, "How many people there are who are one thing at home and something quite different outside! In their homes they have themselves waited on like Eastern potentates; outside they live lives of devotion to others. Authoritarian, tyrannical and argumentative at home; patient and conciliatory in the outside world. Silent and unapproachable at home; chatty and companionable outside. . . .

"So we are all afraid of reality," he says. "We pretend to know ourselves. . . . It is not only the picture other people have of us that we are afraid of having to revise, but also the picture that we ourselves have of other people. . . ."

So "Harry the welder" and those like him must come to grips with it. They need not feel they have missed the boat.

For one thing, as Francois Mauriac put it, "No one can look at himself except down on his knees, in the sight of God."

Finding Ourselves in God

Harry has to get his eyes off the horizontal long enough to find himself in God, to find that God wants him as a welder as much as he does a man who is a missionary to the lost tribes in the Amazon. There is no need to feel guilt or anxiety about what occupation a man or woman holds as long as there is

63

devotion to God to be the best in that occupation. As Paul said, "The Spirit itself beareth witness with our spirit, that we are the children of God: and if children, then heirs; heirs of God, and joint-heirs with Christ . . ." (Romans 8:16-17).

There is no discrimination with God about heirship based purely on what a man does for a career. It is in terms of what a man is in God that counts—whether missionary, preacher, welder, architect, salesman, or whatever.

To avoid guilt about "not doing more" for the cause, which often comes down inadvertently from other levels, one must concentrate on being for God and not simply doing for God.

This is the real cure for moving out from being a mere "personage" to opening up our true "person." It is amazing how people accept that kind of honesty. A welder need not live with trying to protect an image of a metal sculptor. And Harry did not need to feel shortchanged in being a welder in the first place. "God is no respecter of persons" (Acts 10:34). God does not discriminate on the basis of what a man or a woman does.

No Place for Guilt

Since that is the case, there is no place for guilt simply on the basis of not doing what someone else does. As Paul says, "In every nation he that feareth him, and worketh righteousness, is accepted with him" (Acts 10:35).

Let it stand there. Let every man and woman who owns Him as Lord stand with Him on that. And let no man or woman plant unnecessary guilt, deliberately or by default, concerning the will of God for another person. And let no man or woman take that unnecessary guilt it terms of those who are falsely classed as being "in the boat."

Strip the shackles of inferior being, and that person becomes a person. All false notes disappear. He or she is at last free—free from the guilt of "wrong callings" and free to make the best of what he or she has! Such people have to be the apple of God's eye.

From *How to Enjoy Life and Not Feel Guilty,* by James L. Johnson. Harvest House Publishers, Eugene, Ore. Used by permission.

Chapter 8

Setting Realistic Goals

by Dave Stryker

Background Scripture:
Ephesians 6:1-9; Hebrews 10:24; Philippians 3:14

We live in a goal-oriented society. It is part of the fabric of living to set up goals continually from personal and professional achievement to our own family system. The self-help books have cashed, and crashed, in on this basic need and phenomenon from "Pulling Your Own Strings" to "Dress for Success." Most of these "how-to" books are oversimplistic. However, they carry just enough truth to strike a responsive chord within the individual and become a marketable product for our consumer society.

On the personal level, it is easy to get hooked into the syndrome of striving constantly for self-improvement. A saying overheard a few years ago, "The largest room in the world, is the room for self-improvement," plays into this obsession. We are socialized early to be competitive. To be "number one" is chanted from the local basketball team to our national Olympic teams. Within balance, it rightly suggests local and national pride.

©VOLK

66

The tendency is to set up high standards and expectations for ourselves and others. What happens when they are too high or too low? I am suggesting that a tension occurs when we go to one or the other extreme.

Expectations Afoul

I remember when my son was playing little league baseball, and I assumed the role as father-coach for the team during the active summer of an eight-year-old. One of our team members while at bat in the eighth inning with two of his teammates on base, Johnny* was trying desperately to hit the ball, but kept hitting the air. Over the crowd I could distinctly hear his mother shout "Come on Johnny! Come on Johnny!" There was more command in her voice than encouragement. The first two balls were fouled off. When he struck out she jumped down from the stands, marched up to the batter's box, grabbed him by the arm, and half dragging him, scolded him all the way to the car and probably home.

I have reflected on this incident over the past six years and I can still visualize the overanxious mother and the utterly humiliated son on the baseball field. The embarrassed boy never did come back to play on the team.

I have observed parents inflicting their goals and expectations by applying undue pressure on their children—a heavy burden to fulfill some kind of goal that they may not have achieved as a child. This smothers the child's identity by attempting to use them. It violates their personhood rather than validates them as a worthwhile person. During a counseling session with a depressed 14-year-old boy the other day, Jim said, "I did not reach a passing mark on my midterm the other day. I only received a 'D.' I went home to talk to my parents and they ripped me up one side and down the other. I wanted to run away. I felt alone. I felt degraded." Jim was correct in his feelings in that he was degraded because he did not make the grade in their eyes. He was not accepted as a person, nor allowed to fail. Jim felt he could not be worthwhile since he

*This is not his real name. All names in this article are changed to protect the identity of the persons.

was not coming up to their expectations. His parents had no faith in him as a valuable person.

Giving permission for the child to fail may be the most important goal the parent may have; to listen and try to understand the child and the event can be a learning experience for each one on the journey of living together.

Goals

Many times we see in our children a reflection of our own weakness. We do not want them to do poorly in school, as we may have, so we "mirror back" our feelings of hurt, anger, and disappointment. We look for perfection in our children and, not seeing it, we reflect back to them some of our own weaknesses and shortcomings.

Personally, I have found that setting unrealistic goals leads to frustration and tends to contaminate both myself and relationship with others.

I have observed in myself at least three ways of reacting to this frustration. One way I deal with my frustration is to direct it toward others, to externalize my own failure and sense of self-esteem. Sometimes the other person—children, partner, colleagues—takes the full brunt of the frustration and wonders what caused the intensity of my action. Another reaction is to direct the feelings of frustration toward myself. I smother my feelings. By not reaching my goals I can take my frustrations out on my own body with the result of all kinds of psychosomatic complaints. I am internalizing my frustrations. I can develop tension headaches, ulcers, skin problems, and the numerous bodily reactions to the stress of not ventilating (expressing) my feelings.

A third response is to isolate myself from others; to avoid the conflict of not meeting my goals and withdraw. I need private, "alone" times. But withdrawal over long periods can be unhealthy.

What happens when I cannot reach my goals? I sense we can use one or all three of the responses suggested above. A positive response is to take a realistic look at where the frustration is coming from. Am I setting up unrealistic expectations, and goals for myself and others? Are my goals clear and concise with some latitude or flexibility to change the time structure?

Let me illustrate. A parent just returned to school after an absence of 10 years. He was frustrated in that his goal was to receive an "A" but was only receiving a "C." As we talked he revealed that he normally received top grades and was discouraged. He started to take out his frustrations (external) on his children, as well as anyone else who happened to be close to him. After a lot of discussion, he reflected on the other demands on him—his job, his life work, his family were as opposed to him going to school as they had been 10 years previously. After talking about the undue pressure he was putting on himself, he started to look at a more realistic goal which could be implemented over a period of two semesters. By starting with a "C" he would live at "C" level this semester (excuse the pun); he would work toward a "B" for next semester and strive to achieve an "A" the following one. His attitude and perspective changed as he gave himself freedom to moderate his expectations and goals.

When we set up unrealistic expectations, we sense feelings of failure, pain, isolation, and disappointment.

As a parent, I have to work on the balance to encourage my children but also not to expect the impossible. If I have a clear set of expectations and this is specifically communicated to them, generally less frustration takes place.

Give Love

The following event happened last week in an elementary school. While the teacher was instructing her second grade class, she asked them a series of questions: "What is the most important thing in the world to you? If you could have whatever you wanted, what would that be and what would you trade to get it?" Joe, aged seven, replied, "What I want is love . . . and I don't have anything to trade for it. My daddy says I have to earn love but how can I earn love? . . . But God loves me, whether I'm good or bad!"

By helping the person develop realistic goals that can be reached before moving to harder ones, parents can be the channels of God's redemptive love. Otherwise we can set them up for failure.

Provoke Each Other

We are commended in the scripture to "provoke each other." You may reply, "Well I just did that—I provoke a lot of people—I just provoked my friend, or my children!" The biblical statement is not a negative but a positive Word.

Paul was not using the word *provoke* in a negative sense, but as to arouse or initiate. We are "to provoke [each other] unto love and to good works" (Hebrews 10:24). In a positive sense, the *New International Version* suggests, "And let us consider how we may spur one another on toward love and good deeds."

As a family member I can encourage my child and others to love themselves and others in daily relationships. Our families become a microcosm of the world. If we have a sense of self-importance, this is reflected in our daily encounters in the larger world family.

Every family has spoken and unspoken sets of expectations which need to be realistic. Unrealistic goals lead to frustration. Only as I recognize the pressure it puts on me can I start to recognize the demands it places on others. Realistic goals lead to a stronger sense of self-esteem and confidence which equips the person to effectively minister to others.

Chapter 9

Growing in Community

by Thomas L. Goble

*Background Scripture: Genesis 2:18;
Matthew 5:23-24; 6:10; Mark 12:33; Ephesians
2:21-22*

The Bible is a call to community. The key idea is the concept of relationships. In the Garden of Eden God looked over His creation and declared that "it is not good for the man to be alone" (Genesis 2:18),* and so He created woman and the first community began.

The idea of community expanded throughout the Old Testament from the family in community to "The People of God" in community.

In the New Testament, the *ecclesia* ("the called out ones") were declared to be "The body of Christ" (1 Corinthians 12:27) and like a "building . . . being built together" (Ephesians 2:21-22). The Scriptures end pointing to an eternal community, "the city . . . whose architect and builder is God" (Hebrews 11:10). Human experience bears out the fact that man was made for and yearns for life in community.

*All Scripture quotations are from *The Holy Bible, New International Version*.

71

However, the biblical insight as to this basic need for man to live in community, and the clear call of Scripture to the Church to come together in community, must be set against the backdrop of the society in which we find ourselves living and seeking to serve our Lord.

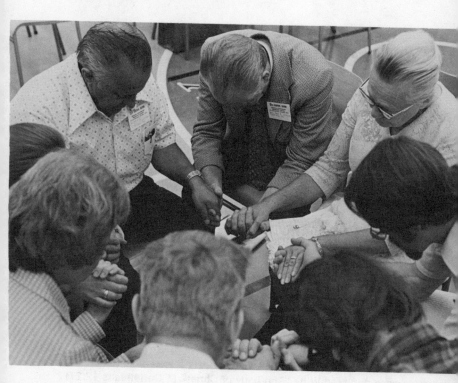

We live in an uprooted society. Frequent moving, separation from one's larger family unit, the depersonalization of urban living in which people find themselves living in anonymity from their neighbor next door or in the apartment across the hall, the fragmentation of the family unit, and the lessening of individual responsibility, all lead to a paradoxical situation.

On the one hand, man has a basic need for community. One cannot live successfully in isolation. There is in life in community, security and fulfillment that cannot otherwise be experienced.

On the other hand, these strong forces at work in our society lead to feelings of isolation, estrangement, and worthlessness.

If one looked at our world only from the perspective of current conditions, the subject of growing in community would present a rather dismal prospect. However, the call of Jesus is to a new order, a new community. The very conditions of our day present one of the most exciting opportunities for Christ's people to offer an alternative that truly is a saving invitation.

The challenge to the church today is twofold. First, how do we communicate to a world living in growing alienation and isolation that there is a community in which one can grow in self-esteem, security, and interpersonal relationship? Second, how can the church keep out the influences of the times that would produce the same fracturing and isolating factors that would dismember the "body" and destroy the "building"?

How can we build a sacred community in a secular world? How can we be a caring-sharing-giving-loving community in a grasping, self-seeking world?

All growth in the Christian community is in relationship to Jesus Christ. In Christ, all share a common source of life. Each one is redeemed by Christ. The active relationship to Christ as the Head of the Body draws all the community into a sense of unity. Jesus declared, "When I am lifted up . . . I will draw all men to myself" (John 12:32).

The vertical relationship is coupled with the horizontal relationship that the community of believers share in the carrying out of our Lord's redemptive work. Common goals, as well as common cause, serve to build community. The sharing in the life of God, as well as the love of God, builds a sense of unity and brotherhood. The command to love God "with all your heart . . . understanding . . . strength" is joined to "love your neighbor as yourself" (Mark 12:33).

The vertical and horizontal relationship to God and others fulfills one of man's basic needs—the sense of belonging and of being loved.

One of the church's primary tasks is to reinforce the sense of belonging to God and the family of God. In that relationship God is love, and I love you, my brother or sister in Christ.

To an insecure world, the church also has the inviting message that faith in God alleviates anxiety and fear. In the Christian community there should be a trust commitment to God and to one another. It is an atmosphere in which one becomes not only convinced that he is under divine protection and provision, but also that the community itself provides support and *security.* To the extent that we can believe and trust in God and believe and trust in each other, to that extent will the community be one of growing confidence and security.

The Christian community grows when it begins to be authentic. This means willing to be vulnerable, open, honest, and truthful—to really believe that in the fellowship of believers I am accepted "warts and all." That which I can see demonstrated beyond superficial sentimentality, an honest love that really hurts when I hurt and celebrates when I succeed, is a growing community—to be open enough to say, "I love you"; to be honest enough to be willing to confront me with my blindness and needs—that is a growing community of faith. The feeling of trust, knowing that my name and reputation are safe with you, provides a community of growth and freedom.

Another aspect of the community of faith is the need for accountability. I am responsive to you as my brother. A basic need in man is the need to feel worthwhile and valuable. Not only do I need to feel my need for you, but I must feel a responsibility to you. I am accountable both to become by God's grace all that He wants me to be and to assist you in becoming, by God's grace, all that He would have you become.

The power of community in Christ is not found in our creeds but in our love. The relationship to a loving God, which in turn releases His love through us to others, produces growth in community. It is a self-giving love which produces trust and community. The response is not one of coercion but of voluntary compliance.

Holding us to such a high ideal has inherent dangers. The world, viewing from the outside, expects Christians to become saints automatically. The cry of "hypocrisy" is often heard as the microscope of examination is held up to the Christian community. But the members of the Body of Christ are quick to acknowledge that "we have this treasure in jars of clay" (2 Corinthians 4:7). The Christian community works through personality conflicts, inferiority feelings, and insecurities. There is a sign along the road, "God is at work!" We have not arrived—we are journeying together. It is the trip that is exciting and the journey together that builds community. We are moving toward a clear-cut objective, "Until we all reach unity in the faith . . . and become mature, attaining to the whole measure of the fullness of Christ" (Ephesians 4:13).

The major distinguishing mark of community for the Christian is the concept of worship. The Christian community is a worshipping community. In a sense, caring, loving, belonging, working, and sharing can be conducted on a strictly human and secular level. Worship is fundamentally an experience of community and is uniquely provided in a religious setting. God offers to man reconciliation and adoption into His family, which produces a sense of belonging and great worth as we recognize the great love of God for us. The relationship that results places the individual in partnership with God in building His kingdom. These individual values, when shared in community, build self-esteem. Worship leads to insights both to ourselves and others, and the kind of relationship that develops produces growth. Real worship confronts us with our relationship in community. Do I truly love my neighbor? Who is my neighbor? Am I in right relationship with others? Jesus went so far as to say, "If you are offering your gift at the altar and there remember that your brother has something against you, leave your gift there in front of the altar. First go and be reconciled to your brother; then come and offer your gift" (Matthew 5:23-24). In community worship, the possibility is offered of the person and community growing simultaneously. This produces a growing sense of community as its members become more and more aware of their potential—the image of God. This is the highest contribution to healthy self-esteem.

Self-esteem is finally realized as one functions effectively in community. "We are saved to serve." One of the points of alienation today is the sense of worthlessness in the day of the "superstar." "We're number one" is the hue and cry of the world. The mad scramble to the top of the ladder leaves all below the top rung feeling, "my best is not good enough." The affirmation of the gospel is that every member has a gift and that gift is vital to the whole. This builds self-esteem. The servant concept elevates all to a common level. My gift is a grace gift. By itself my gift may not be worth much, but as a part of the whole it is vital. This conquers the feeling of isolation, for I am now connected. I am needed. I am important. I am in fellowship and community because we function together in Christ. I am not inferior to others and their gift, for we have all received our gift from Christ. We depend on each other, as we depend upon God.

This combined, gifted community then turns outward in service to carry out God's redemptive work on earth. Self-esteem is discovered in exciting dimensions at this point. It changes the attitude radically from "How can I grow?" to "How can I give myself to you?" "How can I help?" At this point Jesus is heard to say, "Whoever finds his life will lose it, and whoever loses his life for my sake will find it" (Matthew 10:39). To the extent that the community becomes involved in service, to that extent is genuine and full self-esteem discovered. This is accomplished through a unique characteristic of Christian community, *agape* (love). There are no strings attached to this manner of giving. It does not mean the absence of pain, it is the way to the Cross. It is the way of joy. This way of love means sacrifice and suffering, but it is redemptive and thereby fulfilling. This service expresses itself through forgiveness and acceptance. In submission to Christ and one another, we are set free to serve.

A much-needed ingredient is the ministry of affirmation. This means to acknowledge and compliment the worthwhile qualities in one another. This ministry of encouragement is vital to the maintenance of morale and growth. While realizing that we are in fact affirming the grace of God that is operable in our lives, it is nonetheless important to be affirmed on the human level too. While striving for perfection, one must remember to balance praise with constructive criticism.

Appreciation is part of affirmation. Remembering to say, "Thank you," for a kindness received or, "That was helpful," for a ministry enjoyed strengthens the sense of oneness. The closer knit the community becomes, the greater the danger to take one another for granted.

Perhaps the most difficult aspect of affirmation in our competitive world, is to genuinely share in one another's victories and successes. There is no legitimate place in the family of God for sibling rivalry. An atmosphere of affirming love truly produces a growing, Christian community.

The final indicator of full Christian community is openness. The ability to freely say, "I need you." I need your love; I need to say it and hear you say it. This cuts across the grain of our secular world which teaches self-sufficiency and that confessing such a need is a sign of weakness. We are taught to keep our problems to ourselves.

The Christian community admits to weakness. We are created to be dependent upon God and upon each other. This is what community is all about.

Growth in community requires sensitivity to the Holy Spirit's guidance. He will lead us to affirm, serve, trust, and love one another openly in such a way that an observing world can see God's "kingdom come, your will be done on earth as it is in heaven" (Matthew 6:10).

Chapter 10

Acting On Impulse

by Walter Albritton

Background Scripture: Matthew 14:28; 26:33-35;
Mark 11:24; 1 Thessalonians 5:19

For 20 centuries men have claimed that Matthew 14:28 re-
veals a basic weakness in Peter's character. So Peter takes a
licking every time we read this story.

William Barclay does admit that there are "worse sins"
than Peter's trait of impulsiveness. He excuses Peter on the
basis that his "whole trouble was that he was ruled by his heart."
Nevertheless, Barclay voices the standard criticism when he
says: "Peter was given to acting upon impulse and without
thinking of what he was doing. It was his mistake that again and
again he acted without fully facing the situation and without
counting the cost. He was to do exactly the same when he
affirmed undying and unshakable loyalty to Jesus (Matthew
26:33-35), and then denied his Lord's name."[1]

The critics are right, of course, but is there not another side
to every coin? Must we not admit that there is some merit in

acting on impulse, especially when our action is in response to the Lord himself?

While we do not want to go so far as to praise irrational behavior, it is not true that we must often act on impulse if we are to consistently obey the Holy Spirit? Surely many deeds of love and mercy would be left undone if we never acted impulsively in response to what we believe to be the leadership of the Spirit!

Obedience to His Spirit is not always a matter of cool calculation or a calm, rational response to what we know is the will of God. Sometimes we are not sure about His will. Sometimes we are not sure in what direction He wants us to move. This is where faith comes in. As with Abraham, often we must move out not knowing our destination, discovering only upon arrival that we have made the correct decision.

Allowance for the impulsive deed of faith is even more necessary because of the manner in which the Holy Spirit works in our minds and hearts. His voice is usually more of a whisper than a shout. He does not push or shove us into obedience. Rather, He nudges us. And His is a gentle nudge. Most of us know the disappointing pain of having failed to recognize His gentle nudging, discovering to our sorrow that we missed an opportunity to do His will. The impulse was there; but we resisted it, settling for "rational" behavior rather than daring obedience. So at least one mark of Christian maturity is the development of this capacity to recognize the gentle nudging of His Spirit, so that we may more consistently do His will.

I cannot help but wonder how many blessings might have passed me by had I never acted impulsively in response to what I interpreted as nudgings of His Spirit! My wife and I attended the first Christian Ashram held near Orlando, Fla. There we heard E. Stanley Jones for the first time. I went as a troubled preacher, struggling in my first appointment out of seminary, longing for that sense of assurance that John Wesley found at Aldersgate.

I had the "impulse" to talk privately with Brother Stanley (the title he preferred) but almost dismissed it. After all, I was a preacher; having assurance was supposed to be one of my credentials. I was fearful that admitting my need to Stanley Jones would be embarrassing and painful. But like Peter I threw caution to the wind and acted on impulse, and what a blessing resulted!

Sharing my need with Brother Stanley, I was surprised at his understanding and simple response. Quietly he asked if I believed in the promises of Jesus. Of course I did. Then he said, "Let's claim one of them for your need." He quoted Mark 11:24, the words of Jesus: "Whatever you pray about and ask for, believe that you have received it, and it will be yours." We knelt together and he prayed that God would give me the assurance I wanted; but more than that, he thanked God that I had received it! Now, more than 15 years later, I can testify that my need was met completely and His stabilizing assurance continues to fill my heart. But think what I would have missed had I not acted impulsively!

When I was pastor of the Government Street United Methodist Church in downtown Mobile, people frequently walked in off the street and joined our worship services. One Sunday night a woman who was quite drunk came in and sat down on the back pew. This happened shortly after the service had begun. She soon began to make her presence known by asking questions in a loud voice. The congregation froze, no one looking back at her but most of them smiling or chuckling softly.

Finally one woman, acting I think on impulse, walked back and sat down beside the woman. She spoke quietly to her, put her arm around her, and allowed the poor, dirty, drunken woman to crumple in her arms and cry softly during the remainder of the service. Afterward the impulsive woman learned that our street friend was homeless. A victim of five tragic marriages, she was wandering aimlessly across country. Her name was Gracie.

Gracie's soiled dress smelled like something out of the trash heap, but she was a person in need. The impulsive woman in our church found her a place to sleep, helped her get a bath and some clean clothes, sought to encourage her to hang on, and assisted her with a ride to the home of her relatives. We do not know, but perhaps Gracie has turned around and found herself. This we do know; the woman who acted on impulse, reaching out in love to Gracie, has never regretted her action! Others sat cowering in their pews, resisting perhaps the impulse to help. One woman moved quickly, without thinking. In this she was much like Peter. Perhaps we might call her the Good Samaritan Woman—impulsive, but obedient!

One day a man walked into my study without an appointment. He explained, "I was sitting at home thinking about my problem when it occurred to me that I should come talk with you." We shared together as he confessed sins committed more than 20 years before. "I'm not sure God has forgiven me, and I don't have peace in my heart about all of this," he said. He needed to hear a brother affirm God's forgiveness, and to see in a brother's eyes that he was accepted in spite of his sins. God permitted me to be this brother to him, and as we prayed, a wonderful sense of God's peace came to his soul."

In a moment of time, after 20 years of living in anxiety without God's peace and forgiveness, this man on an impulse came to seek out his pastor and confess his sins. How wonderful were the results of his impulsiveness!

It happened during a camp meeting in Michigan. Some of us built a bonfire after the service one night. Around it we sang and shared until almost midnight. Only a dozen people remained when I got up to go to bed. As I walked away, a man rose quickly and suggested we have prayer before retiring. As we got in a circle around the dying campfire, he asked that we pray for him, asking the Lord to heal him of pain in his stomach.

Acting on impulse, I asked him if he knew why his stomach was hurting. As soon as he began to reply, I knew immediately that my question had been prompted by the Holy Spirit. His 20-year-old son had turned his back on his family and his Christian upbringing; he was living a rebellious, wayward life with little regard for the feelings of his father. The father was simply brokenhearted, and he knew that the pain in his stomach was caused by his anguish over his son's behavior. As tears flowed freely down the father's face, all of us in the circle prayed for healing—the healing of the broken relationship of this father and his son. Somehow, in that circle of love in an outdoor setting, we knew that God was answering our prayers!

In a way, we had all acted impulsively, but we had moved toward our Lord in faith. Our obedience had made possible a celebration of love that none of us will ever forget!

I was counseling with a young woman who had very little self-esteem. I had encouraged her to accept her own creativity and to learn to express her deep feelings more. She found it hard to do, especially since her husband often made her feel like a doormat! He ridiculed and teased her unmercifully. Slowly she tried to affirm her own worth and to learn to love herself. Over many months she became a new person, and eventually she was able to write me a beautiful letter.

"After so many years of living in my cocoon I've at last found my way outside and stretched forth my wings to become the beautiful butterfly God intended me to be! It hasn't been easy—finding my way through the outer shell I had so carefully built around my 'real' self. And it isn't easy being a butterfly. But it is the most important reality of my life now. Thank you for being my friend until I could become a friend to myself!"

She probably wrote that letter on impulse, without giving it much thought. But there is no doubt it was a therapeutic exercise in self-expression, enabling her to express her newfound self-esteem. And I was greatly blessed by her impulsive letter of gratitude, for it came on a dreary day when my own self-esteem needed a lift!

So count the cost and think carefully about what you believe to be the will of God for you as a disciple of Christ. But don't be afraid to risk acting on impulse now and then. You may discover with joyful surprise that you are moving in obedience to the gentle nudging of His Spirit!

Meditate for a few minutes on this thought: What impulse have I resisted lately that may well be His gentle nudge?

And consider this: Some joys and blessings will belong to you only when you are willing to act on your impulses. As a beatitude we might express it this way:

Blessed are those who are willing to risk being wrong by acting on impulse, for they shall often experience the joy of knowing they have obeyed the quiet nudgings of My Spirit!

1. William Barclay, *The Daily Study Bible*, "The Gospel of Matthew, Volume II" (Philadelphia: The Westminster Press, 1958), p. 106.

Chapter 11

The Impact of Trauma on Self-esteem

by Jerry W. McCant

Background Scripture:
Leviticus 19:18; John 15:12-13; 2 Corinthians 1:3-5;
Hebrews 13:1; 1 Peter 1:22

Life begins and ends traumatically. Many would agree that few events in life are more traumatic for the individual than birth. Sigmund Freud maintained that death is an intrinsic part of life and should not be viewed as traumatic. Bluntly, he said, "The goal of all life is death."[1] William James speaks for most of us, however, when he called death "the worm at the core" of man's pretensions to happiness.[2] Ernest Becker, in his Pulitzer prize winner, *The Denial of Death,* discussed the universal "terror" of death which underlies all we do.[3]

Furthermore Becker argues that it is precisely this "terror" of death that drives one to heroism as a means to insure his self-esteem. Alfred Adler taught that what man needs most is to feel secure in his self-esteem. He believed that everyone wants to be *Somebody*—someone important enough to be re-

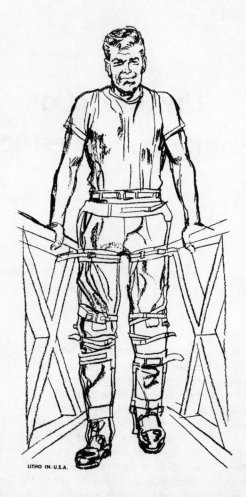

membered, to be immortal. If we care about anyone, we usually care about ourselves first and foremost. As Emerson once said, we would be glad to recreate the whole world out of ourselves.

Freud discovered that each of us, like the mythical Greek god, Narcissus, is hopelessly absorbed with himself. Before condemning it as unchristlike, we should be aware that a healthy level of self-love is inseparable from self-esteem. The struggle comes with the realization that, as Erich Fromm has written, the essence of man is paradoxical; he is half animal and half symbolic or spiritual.[4] Fromm wonders why people do not become insane when they face this tension. There is the symbolic (spiritual) side that gives man infinite worth, but he has a body that is worth about 98c—at least that was what he was worth before inflation! If what has been said thus far is correct, there is certainly a relationship between trauma and self-esteem.

"Trauma" and "self-esteem" are two of those words we use rather freely but have difficulty defining. They are better described than defined. Trauma is generally thought to be negative. Self-esteem is usually conceived in positive terms. Perhaps Becker is right when he insists that all our struggles for self-esteem are really attempts to deny the traumatic, especially the final traumatic event.

Self-esteem has to do with one's perception of himself, his worth, and his place in the world.[5] It relates to his physical appearance, intellect, personality, and most importantly, the feedback he receives from those around him. Other people become the mirror in which he sees his own image. Thus it becomes clear that you are not what you think you are; you are not what people think you are; rather, you are what *you think others think you are!* If a person has a sense of well-being and confidence, we say he has a high self-esteem. When one is insecure, belittles himself, and questions his worth, we say he suffers from low self-esteem. Self-identity is not one's name; it has to do with his dreams, fears, loves, the persons in whom he invests himself.

However we try to define trauma, it is to be recognized as pain. The actual experience of pain is utterly lonely; no one can share it. One person cannot define trauma for another. What might seem minor to one person may be experienced as traumatic for another. "Pain cannot be satisfactorily defined, except as every man defines it introspectively for himself."[6] This was the conclusion of a remarkably comprehensive survey of the scientific literature on pain.

While trauma can neither be precisely defined nor measured for another, there are some characteristics that will help us to understand its nature. Trauma refers to a life-threatening experience as perceived by the traumatized person. Usually, there will be some anxiety concerning object loss—that is, "This is happening and I am going to lose my life, friend, spouse, job, business, etc." One who experiences trauma is forced to accept the "half animal" in himself which Erich Fromm described. He is faced with his own finiteness; he now knows how fragile life really is. Fear normally accompanies trauma, leaving the victim less confident than before.

If one loses a friend in death, especially in an accident which he survives, it may traumatize him. A person who almost drowns or is in an airplane crash will know what trauma is. Divorce is traumatic for many persons experiencing it. Losing one's home in a fire or having a breast removed can be traumatic. Any physical disfigurement or disability (e.g., cancer, amputation, heart attack) may be traumatic. Persons who have been raped or molested and children or spouses who have been battered often feel traumatized. The birth of a handicapped child (physical or mental) may traumatize the parents. War veterans are often the most traumatized of all.

According to Becker, all our heroic deeds are an attempt to earn self-esteem. Those heroic deeds are also a kind of denial of death. Trauma is death rearing its ugly head and facing me with finitude. Being reminded I am "half animal," with feet of clay and worth 98c strikes terror in me. It is the fear of annihilation. Death is absolute negation and any kind of negation (trauma) is a kind of "death." The final scare may be in the hands of the victim, but trauma is always experienced negatively and affects self-esteem negatively.

Most trauma involves the loss of a significant or valued object—part of a body, spouse, child, a family member, or a close friend. "To lose something of this value may be equated, in the individual, with the loss of self. Loss of self is tantamount to the loss of life."[7] When life loses significance and meaning the person begins to die. As the person begins to die, self-esteem plummets and he will feel "small" and may even say derogatory things about himself. Unless something is done to bring healing, this "path of suicide" leads to self-negation and perhaps even to physical annihilation, suicide.

Elizabeth Kubler-Ross has taught us a great deal about death and dying.[8] Her "pattern" for facing death has often been used in discussions about divorce. Since I, following Becker, have seen loss of self-esteem as "dying" and have said that most trauma involves loss of an object, Kubler-Ross' findings might be useful in any discussion of loss. There are five steps in the process:

1. *Denial—Not Me!* Other people get divorced—not me! Some people are raped—not me! Other people die, but the world could not survive without me! I cannot imagine non-being; I will not die. How can I have worth if I am so vulnerable?

2. *Why Me?* I have been good—a good father, provider, citizen, community leader, and a good Christian. Why should I be taken? Why should I be divorced? Why must I, of all people, have cancer? Why must my house burn? Why should my children reject me? There is no justice in this world! Has everyone, including God, turned against me?

3. *Bargaining.* The bargaining involves some other person: often the doctor, the spouse who has filed for divorce, the child who has rejected the parent, even God! The bargaining usually goes, "If you will . . . I will." It is a hope of avoiding or at least postponing "death." One questions his own worth and even his right to bargain.

4. *Depression.* Reality strikes and the person experiences deep depression. There is self-pity, hopelessness, and feelings of powerlessness. It is a "hell" from which there seems to be "no exit." Self-esteem reaches an all-time low—*"I am worthless,"* is the opinion a person has of himself.

5. *Acceptance.* Yes I am going to die, be divorced, lose a part of my body, etc. Out of the acceptance comes the hope that transcends the despair and gives strength to endure and find healing.

Tragically, in dealing with trauma and self-esteem, many do

not come to this final stage of acceptance. They never come to the place where they can relinquish the pain and the loss. For them the loss becomes living death. They cannot relax and joke about something which remains so painful to them. Thus they are consigned to the hell of depression, and there really is little feeling of self-worth in hell!

How does one respond to trauma? Perhaps it will be instructive to see what the symptoms of posttraumatic stress disorders are for Vietnam veterans. The symptoms of the Vietnam veterans serve to illustrate the effects of posttraumatic stress disorders in general. At the same time we realize that there will be differences of degrees in the pain experienced. The symptoms will be similar for anyone experiencing the stress disorders following a traumatic experience. This will, in turn, enable us to see the effects of trauma on self-esteem. For the most part, the effects are negative.[9]

1. *Depression.* Often this is accompanied by feelings of helplessness and hopelessness. Many times the person cries when he talks about his traumatic experience. This can lead to feelings of embarrassment, being exposed to others in his vulnerability. There is the feeling that others do not care and cannot understand.

2. *Isolation.* Depression leads to isolation; the more depressed, the more isolated the individual becomes. Interaction with others is kept at a minimum; it really can be frightening to be with others, especially on a social basis. He neither wants nor feels "worthy" to be with others.

3. *Rage.* This should not be surprising since depression itself is really a form of rage. The anger may become uncontrollable, sometimes in extreme form rendering the person dangerous to himself and others. Fantasies of vindictive retaliation against persons who have wronged him will dance about in his head. In our society, few people having such feelings of rage can have a positive self-concept.

4. *Avoidance of Feelings.* Alienation. This is a kind of emotional insulation. Detached insulation gives some protection against further trauma. If I do not care, I can hardly be hurt! This person is "emotionally dead" and to be otherwise makes him

vulnerable to further attacks. But such an emotionally dead person can have little regard for himself either.

5. *Survival Guilt.* This is particularly the case for war veterans, those escaping from a burning building, accident, earthquake, or tornado. Why was I spared and others taken? Mixed with guilt may also be a death-wish. Dying would have been easier than surviving.

Additionally, persons suffering from posttraumatic stress often experience varying degrees of anxiety. Insomnia is a common complaint. When they do sleep, they often have nightmares. Dreams and nightmares will often be reruns of the traumatic events. Fatigue, depression, anxiety, and stress do little to promote positive feelings about oneself.

Must we leave those whose self-concept has been battered by trauma in the slough of despond? Let us hope not! Research now shows that loneliness and overindividuation aggravated the problem for Vietnam veterans. They went to Vietnam alone, fought alone, returned home alone. There was no unit esprit de corps. Paul teaches us in 1 Corinthians 12 that the Church is a Body. If one member suffers, all members suffer. No one should be allowed to suffer alone.

Maria Anne Hirschmann says that "We Evangelicals are the only group who shoot their wounded!"[10] This is an overstatement but contains enough truth to demand our careful attention. Sometimes the traumas which cause the "death" of self and loss of self-esteem are matters the church condemns. For instance, the church condemns divorce and it should. But, please, don't shoot! The divorced are already wounded. They need love, understanding, and tender care; they do not need condemnation! Healing can come if the church will respond in love.

Few people in the church know how to care deeply on a sustained basis. It is not just a matter of not caring, it is a matter of not knowing how to care. Perhaps we think caring means condoning the person's behavior. It does not. We must learn to care for the person who needs us regardless of our own opinions about his behavior.

Probably it is fear that keeps us from ministering to the

wounded; it will cost me something in terms of pain and involvement. Also if I get too close to a divorced person, it frightens me that it might happen to me too! For that reason, I insulate myself and satisfy myself with telling my brother in the pangs of "hell" that I will pray for him! We must not use prayer as a cop-out! If my brother needs me, I must go and suffer with him.

Remember that it takes a long time for some trauma victims to heal! Their egos are battered and bruised; emotionally they are dead. They have no feelings of value or worth. But God's grace is still a factor to be reckoned with! As a church we must provide rescue teams for our trauma victims. We cannot exempt our soldiers from being wounded but we can lower the casuality rate!

Please allow me a personal note in this discussion. In half-jest I have suggested that I was asked to write this chapter because I have had more trauma and less self-esteem than anyone in the church. I have no complaints about the church but I am concerned that we learn to accept and save our wounded.

Two years ago I *was divorced;* I did not want to be and fought desperately. The church must realize that some of us have no choice! That began a long series of traumatic events— leaving my home behind, having my wife of 16½ years divorce me, suddenly having children "visit" me, having accusations of every sort hurled against me. I have died a thousand deaths and I can tell you that trauma is to self-esteem what a train is to a tomato can on the tracks! It is not over and I have not yet won the battle.

I have experienced friends growing weary of my traumatic fallout. I learned what it was to have friends just "forget" to include me because I was single. A few church leaders have been very condemning in both attitudes and words. Sometimes "friends" have been honest enough to say they can no longer afford the price of my friendship because "It hurts too much." I know about sleepless nights and recurrent nightmares. I know what it means to cry into my pillow in the middle of the night. I know about the pain in the pit of the stomach that never leaves. Paul's statement, "I count it all dung . . ." (Philippians 3:8) has been paraphrased, "I count myself dung," to fit my own situation. In my experience self-esteem falls proportionately with the rise in traumatic stress.

History reminds us what can happen to a person who is poor, ugly, untrained, and unlovable. Despite his high I.Q. he failed at everything. He was rejected by his mother and by his own peers. He was rejected by his country (the Marine Corps) and finally by his foreign-born wife. His wife laughed at him for his inability to supply the family's needs; she made fun of his sexual impotency in front of a friend. The next day Lee Harvey Oswald, the rejected, unlovable failure, killed the man who, more than any other man on earth, embodied all the success, beauty, wealth, and family affection which he lacked. I am not suggesting that every person experiencing trauma will assassinate the President of the United States. I am suggesting that such persons need the grace and support of the church.

Yes, the church can help those who have experienced trauma and the subsequent loss of self-esteem. "Indeed," David Bakan says, "one might well argue that one of the major psychological uses of Christianity has been to overcome the essential loneliness and privacy of pain."[11] Pain, traumatic pain, is individualized and private, but the church must see that it is not borne alone. The suffering person must be reassured of our unconditional love, total acceptance, and constant support. As one works through the grief of his trauma, the church must keep him aware of his work. He is "half animal" and thus finite and fragile. But even under attack he remains "half symbolic" (he has a name and life history) with infinite value. When we have been comforted, we are called to comfort others (2 Corinthians 1:3-5).

Through the funeral ritual, survivors have a vehicle for working through the grief process. The church needs to find ways to help other traumatized persons find healing. It will call for openness, honesty, and acceptance if we are to provide healing for broken hearts. In addition, we must enlist and train people to care. Hurting individuals who are suffering from loss of self-esteem need willing, sensitive listeners, not necessarily professionals. They will need to learn to care deeply on a sustained, long-term basis.

1. Sigmund Freud, *Beyond the Pleasure Principle.* Translated by J. Strachey (*International Psycho-Analytical Library,* edited by E. Jones, No. 4). London: Hogarth Press, 1950, p. 24.

2. William James, *Varieties of Religious Experience: A Study in Human Nature,* 1902 (New York: Mentor Edition, 1958), p. 281.

3. Ernest Becker, *The Denial of Death* (New York: The Free Press, 1973, especially chapter 2), pp. 11 ff.

4. Erich Fromm, *The Heart of Man: Its Genius for Good and Evil* (New York: Harper and Row, 1964), pp. 116-17.

5. For a good discussion of self-concept, see Marie J. Driever's essay in chapters 11 and 12 of Sister Callista Roy, *Introduction to Nursing: An Adaptation Model* (Englewood Cliffs, N.J.: Prentice-Hall, Inc., 1976). See also Virginia Satir, *Peoplemaking* (Palo Alto, Calif.: Science and Behavior Books, Inc., 1972, especially chapter 3).

6. H. K. Beecher, "The Measurement of Pain," *Pharmacological Reviews* 9 (1957), p. 170.

7. B. J. Gruendemann, "Problems of Physical Self: Loss," *Introduction to Nursing: An Adoption Model* (Englewood Cliffs, N.J.: Prentice-Hall, Inc., 1976), p. 194.

8. Elizabeth Kubler-Ross, *Death and Dying* (Macmillan, 1969).

9. For further study, see *Post Traumatic Stress Disorders of the Vietnam Veteran,* edited by Tom Williams (Cincinnati: Disabled American Veterans, 1980).

10. Maria Anne Hirschmann, *Please Don't Shoot! I'm Already Wounded* (Wheaton, Ill.: Tyndale House Publishers, Inc., 1977), p. 105.

11. David Bakan, *Disease, Pain and Sacrifice: Toward a Psychology of Suffering* (Beacon Press, 1971; originally The University of Chicago Press, 1968).

Chapter 12

How Can I Set Others Free to Grow?

by Daniel N. Berg

Background Scripture: Ephesians 4:15;
Philippians 1:6; 1 Thessalonians 5:11; 2 Peter 3:18

Growth is a Christian imperative!

"Grow up in every way, into him who is the head, into Christ" (Ephesians 4:15, RSV).

"Grow in the grace and knowledge of our Lord and Savior Jesus Christ" (2 Peter 3:18, RSV).

The gospel *is* about new birth. But it is also about new life. The task of Christian evangelism is not finished with the birth (conversion) of a new Christian. There is grace to grow!

The Church is a community of Christian growth. It is not now a Church without spot or wrinkle. It could not be. You and I are in it. But it is the Church which Christ loved and gave himself to redeem. He is committed to this community of Christian growth.

The existence of the Bible bears witness to the Christian imperative to grow. One reason for the collection of the mate-

"Therefore encourage one another and build each other up, just as in fact you are doing" (1 Thessalonians 5:11, NIV).

rials of the New Testament by our ancestors in the faith was to provide resources for encouraging growth through Christian teachings. The contents of the Gospel of Matthew are a good illustration. The first Gospel is structured around "memory units" —concise portions alternating between narrative and teaching that could systematically be committed to memory. The essential elements of the life and ministry of Christ could then be carried in the heart and mind of the growing Christian.

References to sanctification and holiness in the New Testament, as they are applied to the believer, express the mature outcome of God's redemptive work. We are not born to remain infants or spiritual children. God is summoning saints—there is grace to grow.

John Wesley was committed to the imperative of Christian growth. There were other revivals underway at the same time in history. But the revival brought by God through Wesley still reverberates because of its commitment to Christian nurture. Until the increasing membership in the Methodist societies made it impossible, John Wesley visited each member of the society at least once every three months. The objective of this personal visit was "to inquire at their own mouths . . . whether they grew in grace and in the knowledge of our Lord Jesus Christ."

Growth is a Christian imperative!

Growth is also "gradual development toward maturity."

Maturity is the objective of true growth. To aid a person in their development toward maturity is to help them grow. To set a person free to grow does not, therefore, mean the removal of all direction from someone else in their development. Hardly any organism in nature grows so rapidly and so freely as a malignant tumor. That kind of growth we call "cancer." It is growth, but it is not healthy growth. Fruit trees will, for a time, grow much lusher and heavier if they are left to develop on their own. But for the production of fruit, pruning is required. The unpruned tree will continue to develop, but not towards its mature end, fruit-bearing. Maturity, marked by wholeness and fruitfulness, is the objective of true growth. To set others free to grow implies the careful direction of their gradual development toward maturity.

Setting another free to grow means providing careful direction. To direct a person seems to contradict the idea of setting him free. In fact, unless our direction is carefully applied it will become a contradiction. The person will either become so reliant upon our advice and direction that his individual growth will be stifled; or, as is more common, the person will simply turn away from us altogether. We must provide direction carefully.

Two considerations ought to give us courage in our attempts to set others free to grow. The first encouragement is that the growth of our Christian brother or sister is motivated from within by the transformation, the renewing, of their minds. We are not working with a person who has no will toward, nor interest in, Christian maturity. The second encouragement is that our Christian brother or sister is directed from within by the Holy Spirit. "I am confident that He who began a good work in you will complete it [bring it to maturity] so that you may be ready for the day of Jesus Christ" (Philippians 1:6, Barclay).[1] The larger part, by far, of directing the growth of our Christian siblings is borne by the Holy Spirit.

We too, however, have responsibility. Our task is "to encourage one another and build one another up" (1 Thessalonians 5:11, RSV). We are to provide direction carefully.

There are some obvious ways in which we can provide careful direction. Other chapters in this book have made some excellent suggestions. We can help others set realistic spiritual goals and work toward them. We can encourage them by evaluating progress made and development yet to pursue. Perhaps, with the growth of trust, we can become agents for accountability. They guide us as we set others free to grow.

But there are less obvious, more subtle areas where we can function as followers of Christ in setting people free to grow. Growth is stifled where there is guilt or guilt feelings; where there is fear to speak the truth about one's deepest thoughts and feelings. When we cannot face ourselves we wither. We are not free to grow.

To help another human being look squarely and openly at himself is, probably, the most important aspect involved in setting another free to grow. It may also be the most tedious, time-consuming, and bewildering thing we can do. In our humanity, even we who have been sanctified wholly can manufacture a complex array of psychological and spiritual mechanisms to obscure our real selves and our deepest anxieties. To help a brother or sister face themselves, whether the vision is gloomy or glorious, is to open them to the liberating power of the gospel and to set them free to grow.

There are no surefire methods to bring a person to the place where he can deal honestly with himself. Sometimes the pain or fear or guilt is just too recent or too intense. But there are some practical and nontechnical approaches to help another find freedom to grow.

Lend an Ear

One way or another, we will find a way to talk about our concerns. Fearing to speak about them to others, we will talk about them to ourselves, either quite literally or in our dreams. We may find that prayer is a way to express our inner selves. The most satisfying way to express our anxieties is to another human being. That we can share the spiritual intimacy of our inner self with another person is one of the great discoveries of late adolescence and early adulthood. Such sharing with a member of the opposite sex lays the groundwork for marriage and family. Whether married or unmarried, however, the desire to find another human being with whom we can make open expression of ourselves is keen.

One would suppose that since trustworthiness or integrity is so important a virtue for the confident, the church would abound with ready candidates. Roman Catholicism has long recognized the importance of the biblical admonition to "confess your sins one to another" and has institutionalized and formalized a procedure for the unburdening of the soul. Protestants as well have created formal procedures for the confession of sins. But these forms become impersonal and can actually contribute to the alienation of the person from the church. The reason is that sins are not the only items that ache to be confessed. Anxiety in all its forms—fear, guilt feelings, failure, worry—all cry out for another human being who will lend an ear. Any of us can do that much, can lend an ear.

Notice, however, that what we are lending is only an ear, and we are only lending it. We may give advice, and because advice is a gift, the recipient is free to take it or ignore it. If we refuse to lend an ear because someone has ignored our advice, we exclude the person from the benefit of our greater service. In most cases, even when a person asks our advice, what they really want is our ear. And then they just want to borrow it. They want to talk to themselves through our ear. They want to

99

hear what they have to say as it sounds in our ear. Surely we can do that for them.

This does not mean that we sit like a post while another talks. It does mean that we might need to reassess our role in hearing what our brother or sister has to say. We are not like spiritual binoculars with extraordinary powers of vision into the distant future of the person to whom we lend our ear. We are, instead, more like a prism that collects the random mixture of hues and tones in the conversation and projects them in a better order so that all the colors, happy and sad, are visible to our friend.

To lend an ear is not simply to assume a passive role. The true listener must be alert to discover and help articulate what the person speaking really wants to tell himself. Far from being passive, to lend an ear is an exercise in intensity.

Have a Heart

Much more serious, and potentially destructive within the church, are the unspoken standards of home and family, of achievement where we work, of spiritual discipline and expectations. For example, discovering that an individual is homosexual can elicit from the church and community the subtle condemnation of the entire family. Marital failures, parent/child problems, and delinquent children create their own unspeakable pain. The church may inadvertently intensify the suffering simply by continually honoring a better standard. Who has not felt the implied guilt that follows when one declines to become involved in a specific area of ministry? To say no for whatever good reasons carries the risk of being perceived as lukewarm or disinterested in ministry in general. Alienation often follows close on the heels of such a decision.

In these and many other similar situations are the acid sources of the wounds of alienation in the church. Ideally the church ought to be the place where such wounds can be healed. In fact, the church, as an institution, cannot do it. But any person who has a heart can.

The last thing bewildered Christian sisters or brothers need to hear is that they are in violation of the unprinted but very real standards of the group of which they are members. They know that already. What they need is a sympathetic setting in which they can discover why they are bewildered and what, if anything, they can do about it.

To set one free to grow means to feel for the heart. To do that, one must have a heart.

Take Your Time

To help another find freedom to grow can consume a great deal of time. Just as there are no surefire methods, neither are there any shortcuts.

Often we try to make shortcuts. For example, we try to help a person see that what he or she is suffering is not unique. Perhaps we reassure the person by confessing that we know exactly what they are describing. There may, in fact, be very little help in this kind of reassurance. Suffering is personal. Misery does not necessarily love company. That perhaps 3 billion people will experience grief during my lifetime does nothing to alleviate my experience of grief. Suffering is personal and requires time and patient listening to deal with it.

There is another reason to take one's time. In private conversations the listening ear may hear its own standards or values being called into question. Reaction is only an impatient slip of the tongue or demeanor away.

Patience will guard the door of the listener's mind so that hasty reaction will be kept out. Suffering or fearful people may deliberately test another's friendship. If the person is defensive and reactionary, the one in pain is not likely to reveal themselves further or become more vulnerable. If the person is open to hear us out, we breathe a sigh of relief and progressively bring to the light our inner selves. Patience makes the listener more interested in the person than in the problems. He or she matters more than heresy or misbehavior or any supposed misdeeds. Patience is taking time to set another free to grow.

Conclusion

Growth is a Christian imperative—the gradual development toward maturity. It is possible where care is given to the direction of another's development. The one who would set another free to grow must willingly lend an ear and have a heart and take his time. Fundamentally, setting another free to grow is not something I can do to or for someone else. It is something I must do myself. I must be committed to the person as a person rather than as a problem. I must be willing to let him hear himself talk through me. I must allow my community and my values to be challenged. And, I must commit all my resources, especially my time, to that one.

1. William Barclay, *The Daily Study Bible* "Philippians—Thessalonians" (Philadelphia: The Westminster Press, 1958).

Chapter 13

How to Handle Success: My Own and Others'

by G. Ray Reglin

*Background Scripture: Genesis 1:27-28, 31;
Romans 12:3; Philippians 4:13; Colossians 3:21*

During the Sunday morning worship hour, Jane had sung a special which inspired many in the congregation and provided an easy transition for the pastor to begin his sermon. Following the service several people commended Jane for the beautiful way she had presented the message of the song and shared what it had meant to them personally. Her response came in quick, short phrases, "It was nothing . . . it was the Lord . . . I should have practiced longer . . . this old dress I have on didn't help me any . . . I missed a note in the third verse. Why can't I do better?" Jane appears to be experiencing low self-esteem. Many of us can identify quite closely with her. Possessing low self-esteem, feeling inferior or inadequate, can be a pressing burden almost too great to bear for an individual.

© VOLK

C. G. Osborne, in his book *The Art of Becoming a Whole Person,* tells of an individual who exhibited positive self-esteem:

> I often think with pleasure of Joe, for over twenty-five years the custodian of the church where I once served. He came over as a refugee after World War II, with his wife and small son. Speaking no English, he was put to work temporarily as janitor until an English-speaking one could be found. But he remained because he became so absolutely indispensable. He learned not only to speak English, but also learned plumbing, carpentry, electrical work, gardening, and a host of other things. Joe may have reached only the seventh grade in the Ukraine where he was reared, but it never crossed his mind to think that he was less important than the Americans who drove Cadillacs. On Wednesday evening he would go home and change clothes. All dressed up he would reappear at the social hall to greet people attending the Family Night Dinner. I am sure that he was more loved than I, and I rejoiced in it because he is a lovable person who accepts himself. He has humility with self-esteem. He loves people and they love him, not only because he is the world's greatest custodian, but because he is a warm, loving person. It would never cross his mind to think of himself as unloved or unappreciated.[1]

Which of these two individuals is the successful person in your opinion? The lady with the beautiful singing voice, who can project the message of a song to an audience, but whose view of herself is so dark and dismal, or the custodian, whose talents lay in being a jack-of-all-trades, and an individual who loves others and likes himself? To answer this intelligently, we need to ask ourselves several questions. First, what is success? Second, from whose eyes is it perceived? Then, what is needed to achieve success and what keeps us from acquiring a high level of success, and finally, what does the Bible say about the topic? The remainder of the chapter will be devoted to answering these vital questions.

What Is Success?

Success for one individual is not necessarily success for another. Success means many things to different people—it may mean securing a particularly desirous job, a new car, being elected to the church board, making money, and on, and on, and on. It can be seen that a definition of success is really a highly individualistic and subjective matter. Success or failure is framed by our personal level of aspiration and is also important to our feelings of self-esteem. To understand how self-esteem is involved with a person's view of success, it might be well to explain what is meant by self-esteem. Self-esteem is a vital part of an individual's self-concept. *Self-concept refers to that particular cluster of ideas and attitudes individuals have about their awareness at any given moment in time. Self-esteem is the affective portion of the self-concept. It involves the feelings and values individuals have about who they are.* These feelings or worthiness/unworthiness determine to a large extent how we define success.

Through Whose Eyes?

The success or failures or even the overall course of our lives may be critically changed by the ways in which we view ourselves. The more we understand our self, the wiser our decisions at every juncture. How does our self-image or self-esteem develop? An individual's feelings about himself have their origin in the early years of childhood, mostly through his interpersonal relationships. The attitudes, points of view, and opinions transmitted to the individual by others, and the identification with other people, all tend to mold the view the individual has of himself. According to Aaron Beck, once a particular attitude or concept has been found, it usually influences future judgments and becomes firmly set. He gives the illustration of the child who gets the idea that he is incapable, as a result of a failure or of being called incompetent by somebody else, and may evaluate future experiences according to this belief. As a result each negative judgment tends to reinforce the negative belief or self-esteem. Thus the vicious cycle is set in motion: each negative judgment reinforces negative self-esteem which in turn reinforces a negative interpretation of future which further consolidates the negative self-concept.

While the foundational base of an individual's self-esteem is rather securely established in early childhood, the individual's later life experiences continue to affect the images and feelings possessed toward oneself. If the mate, friends, and significant others encourage and build up the individual, there is a feeling of an extra positive self-esteem. If the individual lives with frequent criticism, the self-image suffers a great deal. In addition, the individual's life philosophy and religious view also affect the self-concept. Thus it can be seen that others are caught in an intertwined web of influences that unknowingly tie the individual down and frustrate personal growth.

Norman Wright provides a vital link to our understanding of the self-esteem, when he writes:

> It is important to remember that the image a person has of himself *is* determined mostly through his interpersonal relationships. A person's self-image or self-estimate is the result of the *interpretation he makes* of his involvements with others. What really matters to this person is not what others actually think, *but what he thinks they think of him!* It is this subjective interpretation that is important to his self-image.[2]

Success, whatever the definition, usually comes to the individual who generally possesses a good self-image by feeling worthwhile and positive about himself. This person likes himself and is able and willing to accept both the positive qualities and the weak areas of his life. He has confidence in himself, but it's a realistic type of confidence, taking into consideration his limitations. In addition, he has the skill to handle other people's reactions toward him, whether they be positive or negative. He fully expects to accomplish what he is capable of doing and feels that others will respond to him. This type of individual with a positive level of self-esteem has confidence in his perception, ability, and judgment. This results in his being involved in the lives of other people and also opening up his own life to others. Lastly, he is not overly defensive.

What Hinders Our Progress Toward Success?

What hinders individuals from reaching their hopes, their dreams, their aspirations for success? There are certain apprehensions and consequences associated with achieving success, no matter how it is defined, which appear to be an age-old phenomenon which few entirely escape. Hamacheck has noted two possibilities, out of many, why individuals fear success. First, it is likely an above-average amount of success establishes a precedent, a standard to be lived up to, a performance level to be maintained, and this can be very frightening to individuals who have basic doubts about their ability to sustain a high level of personal performance. Second, success may also mean, "I am my brother's keeper." That is, success might be interpreted as having to take care of those less successful, which could be felt as something of a burden. There is a third consideration, which motivates an individual to be less successful than his capacities would indicate, and that is the fear of spiritual pride. This individual tends to zero-in on the badness of man, rather than emphasizing man's goodness through Jesus Christ. The emphasis here is based on negative thinking and a gravitating toward materials which support this view. Two examples which come to mind, are found in Christian hymns:

> *Amazing grace! how sweet the sound!*
> *That saved a wretch like me!*
> *I once was lost, but now am found;*
> *Was blind, but now I see.*
> —John Newton

> *Alas! and did my Savior bleed,*
> *And did my Sov'reign die?*
> *Would He devote that sacred head*
> *For such a worm as I?*
> —Isaac Watts

Hymns such as these can be a wonderful testimony of the life-changing power of God when they form the background for picturing the transformed life. If, however, a Christian sees himself as having no more value than a wretch or a worm, his usefulness to God will be limited and his growth thwarted.

What Does the Bible Say?

The Bible is not narrow, constrictive, or unduly pessimistic but presents a broad panoramic view of life, relative to the development of self-esteem and success. The family plays an important role in assisting the child to establish a variety of concepts and attitudes about himself. The father's role is mentioned in Colossians 3:21 (Amp.):

> Fathers, do not provoke or irritate or fret your children—do not be hard on them or harass them; lest they become discouraged and sullen and morose and feel inferior and frustrated; do not break their spirit.

Parents can and do play an active part in determining the view a young child will have of himself.

Jesus speaks to the issue of the dreadful consequences of a weakened sense of self-esteem when He commands those having contact with small children to deal tenderly with them:

> If a man is a cause of stumbling to one of these little ones who have faith in me, it would be better for him to have a millstone hung round his neck and be drowned in the depths of the sea. Alas for the world that such causes of stumbling arise! Come they must, but woe betide the man through whom they come! (Matthew 18:6-7, NEB).

The implication from Jesus' teaching is clear, those who damage the tender personality of a child have committed a grave sin and will be judged severely.

It appears clear that God intended us to be fully functioning individuals, successful in our endeavors, which in turn, might bring glory to the Father. Several scriptures give credence to this view:

> So God created man in his own image, in the image of God he created him; male and female he created them. God blessed them and said to them, "Be fruitful and increase in number; fill the earth and subdue it. Rule over the fish of the sea and the birds of the air and over every living creature that moves on the ground." . . . God saw all that he had made, and it was very good . . . (Genesis 1:27-28, 31, NIV).

The apostle Paul assists in providing a guideline to use to develop positive self-esteem, when he writes:

> For by the grace given me I say to every one of you: Do not think of yourself more highly than you ought, but rather think of yourself with sober judgment, in accordance with the measure of faith God has given you *(Romans 12:3, NIV)*.

The implication here is that certain guidelines need to be utilized to evaluate ourselves. We are not to think too highly of ourselves. However, by strong inference, it would be most unfortunate to think too lowly of ourselves for this is a negative form of pride. The suggestion by Paul is that we think realistically.

The capstone of positive self-esteem for the Christian is summed up in the words of Paul, when he states: "I can do all things in him who enables me" (Philippians 4:13, RSV). A word of warning needs to be mentioned here before concluding our discussion on success and self-esteem. Maurice Wagner states it well when he says,

> The Bible does not teach that we have a once-for-all sense of inner security as a result of faith in God. Our feelings are variable, for they are reactions to situations. God is constant, we are variable. We may feel very stable and secure today, but tomorrow, with a different set of circumstances, we must continue to choose to exercise faith in Him. By so doing we grow. We do not climb up on a plateau of unchanging inner stability just because we believe in God. We have an unchanging position with Him as His children—that relationship is secured by God's promise.[3]

How does an individual handle success for himself and the success of others? Success achieved by those possessing positive self-esteem and the success of others seem to go hand in hand. Research has rather consistently shown that what we see in others is pretty much what we feel about ourselves. Moreover, there is evidence to suggest that positive self-esteem is reflected by healthy personal adjustment. There is good reason. If an individual thinks positively of himself, then he is more likely to think positively of another. And if the individual thinks positively of another, the other person is more apt to think positively of the individual in return, which has the pleasing effect of reinforcing the individual's positive self-esteem. It is a cyclical process. Friend, be successful in your ventures. Rejoice in the success of others, but do all for the glory of God.

1. C. G. Osborne, *The Art of Becoming a Whole Person* (Waco, Tex.: Word, Inc., 1978), pp. 102-03.

2. H. N. Wright, *The Christian Use of Emotional Power* (Old Tappan, N.J.: Fleming H. Revell Co., 1978), p. 135.

3. Maurice E. Wagner, *Put It All Together: Developing Inner Security* (Grand Rapids: Zondervan Publishing House, 1974), p. 107.